William Shakespeare

# THE TRAGEDY OF
# JULIUS CAESAR

William Shakespeare

# THE TRAGEDY OF
# JULIUS CAESAR

Editor
**Sarah Hatchuel**
*Université de Paris I*
*Panthéon-Sorbonne*

Series Editor
James H. Lake
*Louisiana State University,*
*Shreveport*

Copyright 2008 Focus Publishing

Edited by George Lyman Kittredge.
Used with permission from the heirs to the Kittredge estate.
New material by Sarah Hatchuel used with permission.

Cover Design by Guy Wetherbee | Elk Amino Design, New England.
elkaminodesign@yahoo.com

Cover image: Camuccini, Vincenzo (1771-1844). The Death of Julius Caesar.
Photo Credit: Museo Nazionale di Capodimonte, Naples, Italy. Scala / Art
Resource, NY.

ISBN: 978-1-58510-260-0
ISBN 10: 1-58510-260-1

Printed in the United States of America

10 9 8 7 6 5 4 3 2 1

0507TS

# TABLE OF CONTENTS

## Publisher's Note

George Lyman Kittredge's insightful editions of Shakespeare have endured in part because of his eclecticism, his diversity of interests, and his wide-ranging accomplishments — all of which are reflected in the valuable notes in each volume. The plays in the *New Kittredge Shakespeare* series retain the original Kittredge notes and introductions, changed or augmented only when some modernization seems necessary. These new editions also include introductory essays by contemporary editors, notes on the plays as they have been performed on stage and film, and additional student materials.

These plays are being made available by Focus Publishing with the permission of the Kittredge heirs.

Ron Pullins, Publisher
Newburyport, 2007

## Acknowledgments

I wish to express my deepest gratitude to Dr. Bernice W. Kliman and Professor James H. Lake for their trust; to Professor Pierre Iselin for his seminars on early modern literature at the Sorbonne and to Professor Elisabeth Angel-Perez for her enthusiastic support; to Dr. Nathalie Vienne-Guerrin (University of Rouen), Dr Monica Michlin (University of Paris IV Sorbonne) and Dr. Kevin De Ornellas (University of Ulster) for their scholarly and friendly encouragements; and to Andrée Ganansia, Annie and Fernand Ganem, Isabelle Gonzalez, Nicolas Louvet and Natacha Moenne-Loccoz for always being there.

Sarah Hatchuel
April 2007

# Introduction to the Kittredge Edition

For the text of *Julius Caesar* the First Folio (1623) is the sole authority.[1] The play is exceptionally well printed, and there are few passages where one need hesitate as to the correct reading.

On September 21, 1599, Thomas Platter, a German visitor, attended a performance of 'Keyser Julio Caesare' in a theater on the south side of the Thames. This was in all probability Shakespeare's play, and 1599 may be confidently accepted as the date of composition. Several dramas on Caesar, in Latin, French, or English, were written before Shakespeare took up the subject. "Et tu, Brute?" was not a coinage of Shakespeare's brain. It is a manifest refashioning of the "Thou too, my child?" which Suetonius and Dio Cassius record, and must have become so proverbial that every educated person in the audience expected to hear it when Brutus stabbed Caesar. Shakespeare found the materials for his play in North's translation of Plutarch, in the lives of Julius Caesar, Marcus Brutus, and Marcus Antonius.[2] He has often merely turned North's eloquent prose into his own splendid verse.

*Julius Caesar* opens on the day of the Lupercalia, February 15, B.C. 44.[3] Caesar's triumph, which Shakespeare puts on the same day, was celebrated in the preceding October. The murder of Caesar took place on March 15, B.C. 44, in the Senate House on the Campus Martius. Shakespeare substitutes the Capitol.[4] At the end Shakespeare brings the two battles of Philippi together. In fact, they were about three weeks apart. In the course of the first, which was indecisive, Cassius was killed,

---

1   Folios were large, expensive books. The First Folio, the first complete edition of Shakespeare's plays, was printed in 1623, seven years after Shakespeare's death. Sometimes the Folio versions differ from the Quarto versions (cheaply bound single editions of plays), and modern editors have to decide which version they should present to their readers. No Quarto version of *Julius Caesar* was apparently published during Shakespeare's time, and therefore all editions are based on the Folio.

2   The first edition of Sir Thomas North's translation of Plutarch, from the French of Jacques Amyot (himself translating from Latin), appeared in 1579. The first edition was dedicated to Queen Elizabeth, and was followed by another edition in 1595. North's translation formed the source from which Shakespeare drew the materials for his *Coriolanus, Julius Caesar* and *Antony and Cleopatra*.

3   The Lupercalia was a fertility festival in ancient Rome, celebrated on February 15 in honor of a pastoral god. We may actually owe our observance of Valentine's Day to this Roman celebration.

4   The Capitol was the summit of the Capitoline Hill which overlooked the Forum. It was the site of a temple of Jupiter where triumphs (processions after victories) were notably celebrated.

at his own request, by Pindarus. After the second, in which Octavius and Antony were victorious, Brutus committed suicide. This was in the autumn of 42 B.C.

The structure of the play has often been questioned and the correctness of the title has been challenged accordingly. It is rather the tragedy of Brutus, we are told, or of Brutus and Cassius, than the tragedy of Caesar; and the plot is not unified, for Caesar disappears in the middle of the drama: thus there are two catastrophes— the murder of Caesar and the disaster at Philippi. It has even been suggested that Shakespeare reworked and combined two distinct lost plays—a *Death of Caesar* and a *Revenge for Caesar*. These strictures and this ingenious reconstruction come from ignoring the supernatural, which is as important an element in JULIUS CAESAR as in *Macbeth* and *Hamlet*. There is no lack of unity in the plot. Caesar vanquishes Brutus and Cassius at Philippi as truly as he vanquished Pompey at Pharsalus. Antony and Octavius are not Caesar's avengers: they are merely Caesar's agents; he avenges himself. As Caesar was warned to beware the ides of March, so Brutus, in a speech full of tragic irony, warns Cassius: "Remember March; the ides of March remember."[5] This is at Sardis, in the fourth act, when the real crisis is imminent, and that night the ghost of Caesar appears to Brutus and warns him of what is to come: "Thou shalt see me at Philippi." It was no idle threat. Nor is it an accident that Cassius takes leave of life with the words

> Caesar, thou art reveng'd
> Even with the sword that kill'd thee;

and that Brutus, finding Cassius and Titinius dead, cries out

> O Julius Caesar, thou art mighty yet!
> Thy spirit walks abroad and turns our swords
> In our own proper entrails.

Caesar, alive or dead, pervades and operates the drama—and not less after his death than in his life. Caesar's character, as represented by Shakespeare, has evoked much hostile criticism. How can we accept this pompous, strutting figure, who stalks blindly to his doom, as "the foremost man of all this world"? Is this the conqueror, the wit, the scholar, the mighty organizer whose plans have changed all history? Was the historical Caesar so antipathetic to Shakespeare that he either could not or would not portray him adequately? To answer such questions is not difficult. Caesar's lordly style, his pompous habit of speaking of himself in the third person, has been adequately explained by reference to the Latin tragedy of *Julius Caesar*, by Muretus, first published in 1553. Muretus invested Caesar with the style and manner of Seneca's braggart Hercules, and this device had established a fashion: the audience expected the Caesarian dialect. And, quite apart from the mere question of language, Shakespeare is representing Caesar, not in complete biography, but at the very end of his triumphant career. He has risen so high that he has become the victim of infatuation. It is not Caesar in his best estate, then, that Shakespeare has to bring

---

5    The "Ides" refers to a day in the Roman calendar which marked the approximate middle of the month.

upon the stage, but Caesar drunk with dominion, forgetful of his own mortality—careless, therefore, of the ordinary rules of prudence and self-protection.[3] Whether or not this conception is historical need not concern us. It is easy to find evidence in Plutarch to justify it; and, in any case, it accords with the ancient doctrine of infatuation—that blindness which the gods send upon those who profanely aspire to divinity. It is this self-deification which Cassius finds intolerable (1.2.115-118):

> This man
> Is now become a god, and Cassius is
> A wretched creature and must bend his body
> If Caesar carelessly but nod on him.

The feeling that breaks out in these lines runs through the whole of his passionate appeal to Brutus to save the republic. Cassius acts from mixed motives. It is patriot's duty, he believes, to restore the republic by abolishing the imminent despotism of Caesar. Yet, in his hatred of tyranny Cassius is governed as much by temperament as by patriotism. But this passion does not burn with a clear flame, for his noble scorn of servitude is tainted with ignoble envy. It is Cassius's nemesis that, in winning Brutus, he has merely changed masters. For Brutus, the patron saint of the republican cause, has a fatal quality that often accompanies eminent virtue. Serenely conscious of his own integrity, he is equally certain of the accuracy of his judgment. And Brutus is not, like Cassius, 'a great observer'; he cannot 'look quite through the deeds of men.' He is almost always in the wrong when matters of policy or tactics are involved, and Cassius cannot withstand his serene self-sufficiency. Thus, against Cassius's advice, Antony the avenger is spared and allowed to deliver the funeral oration, and the march to Philippi is undertaken instead of a more Fabian policy.

The soliloquy in which Brutus persuades himself to join the conspiracy of assassination (2.1.10-34) has given critics a good deal of trouble. It is obvious that he is balancing reasons *pro* and *con,* but the details of his mental process require attention. Brutus does not for a moment give up his objection to Caesar's becoming king, which he has already expressed in 1.2.79-82, and reiterates with splendid emphasis in the soliloquy. Here he is considering the question of assassination from another point of view—that of Caesar's personal character, which, he rightly feels, is not such as gives an edge to the sword of a tyrannicide. He finds nothing in his *personal* relations with Caesar, or in Caesar's private character, that justifies enmity; for Caesar is his friend and is (personally) an amiable and high-minded man. But with reference to *the general*—the people at large—the case is different. It is only on *public* grounds, then, that Brutus can justify the murder. And here, too, he feels a scruple; for—though the crown may change Caesar's nature, as it will certainly give him dangerous authority—Brutus cannot deny that he is not unlikely to rule with wisdom and moderation. If, however, he can persuade himself that Caesar's nature will really be changed by the kingship—that he will govern tyrannically—then Brutus can strike at him with a better will. Unlimited power, he reflects, may easily be misused, and the special danger of such misuse lies in the tendency of absolute monarchy to become merciless. True, Caesar has never let his feelings and impulses govern his reason: he has always kept his balance. Yet, when he reaches the summit of his ambition, he may yield to the common temptation of despots and become tyrannical. And this danger, Brutus concludes, justifies the assassination.

Shakespeare is no partisan in this tragedy. He sides neither with Caesar and his avengers nor with the party of Brutus and Cassius. The verdict, if there must be a verdict, he leaves to history. Caesar, by the testimony of Brutus, was 'the foremost man of all this world' (4.3.22); Cassius, by the same testimony, was 'the last of all the Romans' (5.3.99); and the drama closes with a tribute to Brutus, 'the noblest Roman of them all.'

George Lyman Kittredge

## Editor's Note:

I have mainly retained the Kittredge introduction, eliminating only comparisons with the sources and mentions of *Julius Caesar* in other works contemporary to Shakespeare. Explanatory footnotes are mine. [S.H.]

# Introduction to the Focus Edition

I will divide this introduction into three parts—a study of how the play works in terms of structure, themes and gender; a history of the play in performance; and an analysis of the screen adaptations.

## How does the play work?

*Julius Caesar* is one of William Shakespeare's Roman plays. It is a tragedy set in a very specific place and time, that rewrites historical material into an artistic experience, offering a view of Rome from an Elizabethan standpoint. In *Julius Caesar*, time concentration aims at creating dramatic effects—Caesar's ceremonies of triumph (that occurred originally in October, 45 B.C.) take place at the same time as the Lupercal ceremonies (that really happened in April, 44 B.C.); Octavius arrives in Rome on the very day of Caesar's murder instead of six weeks later; the two episodes of the Battle of Philippi happen on the same day instead of being separated by twenty days. But time concentration also creates a sense of doom, precipitating the death of Caesar or the suicides of Brutus and Cassius. In the play, Shakespeare appears to project the Elizabethan fear of chaos onto Roman history. Renaissance England had an organic and harmonious vision of the universe—all creation was ranged in an unalterable order from the angels down to men, and from there to the beasts and plants. In that great chain of being, the ruler held a special place—he represented a crucial link between God and the earth. If the monarch was murdered or if the crown was usurped, chaos and confusion were expected to replace peace and natural order. The character of Julius Caesar seems to stand for the leader preserving the natural order, and his murder leads the Roman Empire into turmoil, in the same way that the civil war of the Two Roses between the adherents of the House of Lancaster and the House of York divided England in the fifteenth century. Caesar's murder conditions the whole structure of the play—all that precedes announces it and all that follows prolongs it in violent aftermaths. If Caesar disappears before half of the play is over, his figure keeps haunting the play like Nemesis, the vengeful figure in mythology. Caesar is almost presented as the equivalent of an anointed English king whose destiny can be read in the sky. With thunder and comets, signs in heaven anticipate Caesar's death and the chaotic future of Rome: "When beggars die there are no comets seen;/ The heavens themselves blaze forth the death of princes" (2.2). In the Renaissance, the movements of the stars and the appearance of comets as well as eclipses were believed to be the origin of disaster. The murder of Caesar is thus presented as a fatal mistake which plunges Rome into political turmoil and civil strife. The order imagined by the conspirators only ends in dangerous disorder, in a social unrest that will lead to the murder of innocent men—as Cinna the Poet is killed instead of Cinna the Conspirator. Moreover, instead of destroying tyranny, the assassination of Caesar only creates more absolutism, leading to the reign of Octavius-Augustus.

In fact, what the conspirators seem to deny is precisely Caesar's representation of the natural order. Cassius, the ambitious malcontent, succeeds in convincing Brutus that his name is as worthy as that of Caesar. Brutus is duty-bound to take sides with the conspirators because he embodies the Republic through his ancestor Junius Brutus, who committed the first regicide of the monarchy and set up the Republic in B.C. 509. However, it is not often mentioned that Junius established a new reign, that of the Patricians—a kind of social elite who soon monopolized political power. In overthrowing Caesar, Brutus does not wish for the rule of the people, but for the return to the reign of the Patricians. In this, he wishes for a revolution in the original sense of the word—a return to the starting point. It is therefore very difficult to apply the modern notions of democracy or fascism to *Julius Caesar*. In the play, Caesar's tyranny is rather underplayed. His human weaknesses, such as his epilepsy and deafness, are emphasized, revealing the vulnerable human being behind the mask of power. Critics have regularly noted the grotesque discrepancy between Caesar's political domination and his physical inferiority. This can be linked to England's own political situation at Shakespeare's time, with a woman, Elizabeth I, at the head of the state. But physical limitation is not the only element that lessens Caesar's tyranny. Even Brutus admits that Caesar's actions have always been governed by reason: "And to speak truth of Caesar,/ I have not known when his affections sway'd/ More than his reason." (2.1).

Points of view keep alternating and changing our vision of the whole play. We, the spectators, are almost in the same position as the crowd that listens to Brutus's speech and then to Antony's oration. After supporting Brutus, the crowd soon allies itself with Antony. The Roman people are thus marked with a tragic flaw—that of fickleness and instability. The crowd, blind and influential, can commit murder without reason—Cinna the Poet is thus lynched through a mere mistake in identity. The tragedy, therefore, does not seem to be that of Brutus or of Caesar, but that of Rome and the Romans. Instead of a domestic, personal tragedy, Shakespeare may have written the political tragedy of a whole empire and its people in a reflection on power and the legitimacy of its conquest. Shakespeare does not make a clear choice between Caesar and the conspirators but revels in ambiguity. He does not present an apology for absolutism or democracy. The freedom that Brutus and his followers pretend to give back to the people is a mere slogan, a word that is simply repeated, empty of concrete meaning and effect: "Liberty! Freedom! Tyranny is dead!," "Liberty, freedom, and enfranchisement!" (3.1).

All kinds of idealism are shown as fragile and dangerous. Brutus finally kills Caesar not for what he is, but for what he could become. In the very name of justice and honor, he murders his benefactor, thus denying the very notions of justice and honor. The conspirators, who, in the words of Cassius, have become "womanish" (1.3) under Caesar's dictatorship, can only be renewed through the assassination of Caesar. They wish to be the walls that will prevent Caesar's political body from invading and overflowing Republican Rome. Caesar's body, as it is invaded by the conspirators' daggers and bleeds involuntarily, is symbolically transformed into a female body that cannot control its menstrual bleeding. Antony soon sees Caesar's wounds as mouths waiting for a voice ("Over thy wounds [...]/ Which, like dumb mouths, do ope their ruby lips/ To beg the voice and utterance of my tongue" 3.1), thus creating a monstrous kind of ventriloquism. When Antony starts to speak to the people of Rome and to the spectators in the theater audience, dead Caesar is resurrected through vocal delivery and the reading of his will. He is turned into an exceptional man and a victim rather than a tyrant. Contrary to Brutus who only uses a very abstract and moral kind of rhetoric, Antony discloses striking, material visions—Caesar's corpse, Caesar's blood, Caesar's will—which makes his whole speech powerful, convincing and almost erotic. It is as though Antony's voice and tongue were now fertilizing Caesar's wounded, feminized body.

If Caesar's corpse becomes female, Portia's own body is masculinized since she replaces involuntary bleeding by a voluntary wound that she bears with patience, like a man. Her body also becomes masculine through Cato, her father, and Brutus, her husband ("Think you I am no stronger than my sex,/ Being so father'd and so husbanded?," 2.1). By presenting herself as manly, Portia wishes to take part in her husband's project and participate in the new, regenerated body politic. To do so, she first has to show that her body is strong and that she is not a "leaky vessel," a term widely associated with early modern English women for their leakiness—they were thought not to be able to hold a secret. However, paradoxically, in order to prove that she does not "leak," she must mutilate herself and bleed in a manly and stoic way.

The words "blood," "bloods" and "bloody" actually appear thirty-six times in the text. The notion of "blood" is linked to life and honor, but also to violence and battle, and no occurrence has exactly the same meaning in the play. Calphurnia's dream (of seeing Caesar's statue bleed) is given two diverging interpretations. Calphurnia says that blood is a sign of death and implies an ill-fated vision; but according to Decius, the vision is positive and announces that Caesar will revive the Romans with his fertilizing, sacred blood. Ironically, the play reconciles the two different readings. Caesar is murdered as in Calphurnia's interpretation, but the Romans will also dip their handkerchiefs in Caesar's blood to turn them into holy relics. In the play, the signs are therefore shown to be reversible—death and renewal are merged into one.

Roman Paganism and Elizabethan Christianity are also combined. While Plutarch reported that Caesar had been stabbed twenty-three times, Shakespeare changes the figure to thirty-three, the age of Christ when he died. Some critics think that this may be a mistake by Shakespeare, but some others believe that the playwright transferred the story of Caesar into a Judaeo-Christian universe, emphasizing the link between Caesar and Christ. Julius Caesar also becomes a Christ-like figure during the ritual performed by the conspirators. As they all plunge their daggers into Caesar's body before washing their hands in his blood, they insert a parody of the Christian Eucharist into the pagan world of Rome. Shakespeare also elaborates a connection between the ritual and theatrical performance, in a metadramatic discourse that reflects on the medium of theatre itself and presents the murder of Caesar as the model for a series of re-enactments that will take place in staged shows or in real life: "How many ages hence/ Shall this our lofty scene be acted over/ In states unborn and accents yet unknown!" (3.1). The text of the play, therefore, anticipates the variety of its performances over the centuries.

## How has the play been performed on the stage?

First of all, it has to be said that the play of *Julius Caesar* has never attracted the leading actors of their age, such as David Garrick, Charles Kean, Henry Irving or Laurence Olivier. It is quite a difficult play to produce for three main reasons: the titular hero dies in the very middle of the play; three other characters compete for the sympathy of the audience; and the populace needs to reach a balanced, appropriate number if it does not want to lose any dramatic power or, on the contrary, mire the whole theatrical event. The directors must be careful to view the play as an *ensemble* drama rather than fall to the romantic vision of a play belonging to a single hero.

The first performance of *Julius Caesar* on record was attended by a Swiss traveler, Thomas Platter, who wrote that he saw the play performed with a cast of fifteen at least. The performance took place on the 21st of September, 1599, probably at the Globe Theater in London, that is to say in open air, on a thrust stage surrounded by groundlings and devoid of any realistic devices such as sets or elaborated props.

After the Restoration in 1660, the theaters became private, indoor and lit by candles. However, theatrical events were still largely based on an intimate relationship between actors and spectators, and did not aim to reach a realistic representation of the action. Thomas Betterton, as Brutus, brought to the part dignity, majesty, reserve and seriousness. From 1684 to 1707, Betterton established a tradition which, for a long time, saw Brutus not only as a philosopher (opposed to a fiery and passionate Cassius) but also as the real hero of the play.

Later in the eighteenth century, the play became less popular and was performed less often. Producers attempted to lessen what they thought to be flaws in the construction of the play by redistributing speeches, and by rewriting or cutting the text (the shocking scene showing the murder of Cinna the Poet was thus totally excised for centuries). The Dryden-Davenant[6] rewriting of the play (which was used during the first half of the century) still highlighted Brutus's heroic, generous and martyr-like qualities. For example, he did not fetch Caesar at his home to bring

---

6    John Dryden (1631-1700) adapted many Shakespeare plays to the tastes of a new audience. He notably collaborated with William D'Avenant (1606-1668), an English poet and playwright.

him to the Capitol; he did not wash his hand in Caesar's blood after the murder; and, finally, instead of being helped to die, he stabbed his own self after having proclaimed his love for freedom and his country. Brutus (played by Barton Booth) thus prevailed on the stage, carrying the play and all its dramatic moments on his shoulders. The mob in the Forum scene was still very small and its exclamations drastically cut to speed up action. Antony did not share Brutus's dignity or his charisma. These choices encouraged a patriotic vision of the play, with Caesar as the oppressing villain suppressing all freedoms and Brutus as the righteous hero ready for everything to restore liberty. This vision was most naturally similar in America, where *Julius Caesar* appealed to the revolutionary fervor of the 1770s. The American Company presented Brutus as a true patriot struggling for liberty and emphasized the necessity of Caesar's death to restore the rights of the citizens.

This interpretation of Brutus reached its peak with John Philip Kemble, who played the part in London from 1812 to 1817 as a blameless, sincere and stoic idealist. He notably restored the play to popular favor by staging it as Brutus's tragedy and introducing visual aids to the audience's imagination—painted backgrounds of Rome, processions and majestic groupings of extras (who numbered close to a hundred). A system of painted shutters was thus developed. They slid along rails to facilitate their placement during the performance, and were positioned on the stage at various distances to create *trompe-l'œil* effects. Kemble also cut the text drastically, eliminating minor characters and focusing mainly on the conspirators (and especially on Brutus's dilemma and tragic course) to give the play more unity. The part of Antony, played by Charles Kemble as a young and noble athlete, started to be enhanced and his motives as calculating opportunist transformed into an earnest desire for justice and revenge after the death of his benefactor. For the first time in the play's history, Caesar's assassination, though staged as an exaggerated, formal ballet with an overplayed Caesar, was actually presented as the play's highest point.

After Kemble's seminal production, the costumes and sets became more and more accurate and sophisticated. From 1819 to 1851, the play was associated with William Charles Macready, an actor-manager who played the roles of Brutus and Cassius alternatively throughout his career. Macready strived for a realistic style of representation, relying even more heavily on lavish sets and letting the crowds of extras take part in the plot much more than in Kemble's production. For the first time, the people of Rome took an active (and crucial) part in the performance. For the first time also, the murder of Caesar was staged realistically (with senators, soldiers and citizens reacting naturally in terror and confusion to the terrifying event) and the spectacular potential of the Forum scene was exploited with the crowd as a vital force of the drama. The play was almost transformed into a convincing domestic tragedy in which the spectators were encouraged to identify with the feelings experienced on stage, especially with those of Brutus, whom Macready played as a tender character with a natural grandeur of soul, as reluctant to do violent deeds as ever, and tragically led into error.

The American productions were as spectacular as the British ones. In the United States, the play enjoyed unmatched popularity between 1871 and 1891, with the three Booth[7] brothers in the main parts. As an actor-manager, Edwin Booth attempted to emphasize the emotional impact of the play over the archaeological accuracy, using complex chiaroscuro lighting effects, as many as two hundreds extras and statuesque groupings in the traditions of romantic realism and nostalgia for a noble past. Brutus was still the hero of the play—even his exit at the Forum scene was emphasized over that of Antony. And at the end, following the English tradition, Brutus stabbed himself tragically. Booth's unfit physique did not allow him to play Brutus as a majestic and strong character, so he chose to present him in a romantic and sentimental way, as a man of pure ideals and poetic sensibility rather than as a man of deeds, waiting to stab Caesar until the very last moment and doing so with extreme loathing and reluctance. As in Macready's production, the assassination scene was made the core of the play, the setting of which was influenced by Jean-Louis Gérôme's 1867 painting *La Mort de César* in its picturesque groupings. This *mise-en-scène* allowed for fluid and natural movements that reinforced the emotional impact of the action and the realism of reactions among the characters on stage.

In England, actor-manager Herbert Beerbohm Tree successfully revived *Julius Caesar* in London—the play had not been produced there for more than thirty years. He hired the eminent painter Lawrence Alma-Tadema to create lavish, more or less historically accurate settings, and staged the play as a spectacular and realistic event with two hundreds and fifty extras for the crowd scenes. Tree was very much influenced by the visually striking production of the Meiningen Court Company which was presented (in a German translation) in London in 1881. The Meiningen production did not favor one role over the other but, for once, viewed the play as an *ensemble* drama. The Forum scene highlighted Antony's demagoguery and his interaction with the mob. This staging changed the course of the performance history of the play as it persuaded Tree that Antony, and not Brutus, was the real hero of *Julius Caesar*. Tree believed that Marc Antony conveyed the whole glamour and strength of the play and might appeal to the audience much more than the delicate Brutus. Significantly, Tree chose to play Antony instead of Brutus or Cassius. In order to impose this new vision and present Antony in a favorable light, Tree did not hesitate to cut the text in a radical way—the Proscription scene (4.1) was, for example, totally suppressed and, after the climax of the Forum scene (3.2), the rest of the play was drastically edited [notably the Quarrel scene (4.3)] to rush to the end and come back to Antony again. The play was now composed of three acts only, which respectively introduced Antony (until Caesar's death), showed him devising his plot (in the extremely impressive sequence of the Forum) and revelled in its final triumph (during the battle). In the assassination scene, the rapidity of the murder emphasized the conspirators' sadistic brutality and savagery. Antony was now

---

7    The Booth family was a British-American theatrical family of the 19th century. Its most famous (and infamous!) members were Edwin Booth (one of the leading actors of his time) and John Wilkes Booth (who assassinated Abraham Lincoln in 1865).

presented as the heroic champion and avenger of a great man unjustly murdered. The fact that Caesar was convincingly played with high dignity and humanity only added strength to this interpretation. But this unambiguous, favorable vision of Antony was not to last long on stage. In 1919, William Bridges-Adams mounted the play in Stratford-upon-Avon with an almost full text (but the Cinna the Poet scene was still missing) and a simple stage, devoid of extravagant effects. This had not happened since the Restoration. With the Proscription scene restored, the part of Antony evolved considerably—the noble athlete suddenly became also a callous opportunist and showed much more ambivalence. This full-text trend went on with Robert Atkins's 1921 London production which again rejected the tradition of realistic set design, using only some white steps and a few columns. This approach combining textual integrity with stagecraft simplicity was to be continued in 1929 by Harcourt Williams, who started to rediscover the virtues of an ensemble drama intricately presenting four hero figures. In 1935, Henry Cass directed another full-text version (with a simple but arresting décor) that featured a very rich characterisation of Caesar at the same time conveying majesty and weakness, splendor and ruthlessness.

Contrary to the full-text British versions, in 1937 Orson Welles presented in New York a radical interpretation conveyed through extreme textual cuts. The Mercury Theater production was quick, fluid and violent, using lights and sounds in a very expressionistic way. Welles chose to convey a contemporary political vision by drawing parallels between Caesar's dictatorship and the rise of Fascism and Nazism in Europe. The play was therefore subtitled "The Death of a Dictator" and performed in modern costumes. Antony was the archetypal opportunistic hypocrite, while Brutus was played as an intellectual liberal trying to act against despotism but not knowing exactly how to act. As he is unable to beat tyranny with its own weapons, such as violence and demagogy, Brutus vanquishes his own idealist cause and leads the way to even more authoritarianism. To offer this strong vision, Welles cut so much from the text that the play, lasting now less than two hours, was almost turned into a film script, with very suggestive cinematic effects achieved through alternations of light, darkness and shadows. Welles notably emphasized the violence at work in the play. The Forum scene was made to resemble Hitler's rallies at Nuremberg, while the episode in which Cinna the Poet is savagely lynched was not only included, but also augmented with lines taken from *Coriolanus,* and turned into one of the production peaks.

Welles's radical production rapidly influenced *mises-en-scène* in England. In 1938, Henry Cass directed the play again in order to denounce the struggle between modern idealism and power supported by an uncritical public. However, unlike Welles, he did not cut much of the text. To convey his anti-Fascist vision, he only relied on natural speaking and modern costuming (such as SS uniforms for Antony and his allies).

The first major post-war performance of *Julius Caesar* took place in Stratford-upon-Avon in 1950, with an elaborate setting and a cyclorama showing changing skies according to the mood of the scene. John Gielgud played Cassius and, for the first time in the play's history, brought complexity, nobility and vitality to the part. Seven years later, Glen Byam Shaw saw Brutus as a combination of heroic nobility and poetic sensibility and presented Antony as a magnetic, passionate and sincere man who becomes progressively aware of his spellbinding skills and turns ruthless. Most importantly, he put the character of Caesar right at the core of the play. Trevor Nunn's 1972 production for the Royal Shakespeare Company also saw Caesar as the play's pivotal figure—a tyrant striving for divinity. The murder scene thus became a responsible act of citizenship.

Modern stage productions, apart from presenting more or less realistic or impressionistic Roman settings (see Peter Hall's 1995 RSC production), have also turned to recreating an Elizabethan style or to finding contemporary equivalents to dictatorial tyranny. It has thus become customary to see some *Julius Caesar*s drawing parallels with Castro's Cuba, Mussolini's Italy or Ceausescu's Romania (see David Thacker's 1993 RSC production). Despotism has often been emphasized by placing a huge statue or image of Caesar looming overwhelmingly and dominating the stage as well as the characters' psyches (see Peter Hall's 1995 production). The crowd has been either absent and represented acoustically through sounds of cheering (as in Terry Hands's 1987 RSC production), or with dozens of extras. Performances often work on the mob's facelessness, fickleness and unpredictability. During the 1999 production at the London Globe Theater, extras were placed among the groundlings to try and stir the audience into more interaction with the actors. Violence, blood and callousness have also be essential features of recent performances. The murders of Caesar and Cinna the Poet often end in horrifying bloodshed, while Antony is regularly presented as an archetypal calculating villain. There is no doubt that the cinematic medium is now influencing the way the play is presented.

## How has the play been adapted to the screen?

*Julius Caesar* has provided source material for many film and television productions. Silent versions of the play had been made in the US (1908), Italy (1909) and Britain (dir. F. R. Benson, 1911). The first talking version was directed by George A. Cooper in 1926 to highlight *DeForest Phonofilm*'s then-new synchronized sound system. As with the Benson production, it now appears to be lost. Four films using Shakespeare's text are widely available—David Bradley's independent, low-budget, but highly cinematic 1950 version; Joseph Mankiewicz's 1953 Hollywood movie; Stuart Burge's 1970 epic experience and Herbert Wise's 1979 full-text staging for the BBC.

Bradley's 1953 film, though very limited in its budget and shot in 16 mm, is extremely inventive in its handling of black and white to create expressionistic effects. The film is composed of two parts, made explicit through two intertitles: "The Murder of Caesar" and "The Revenge of Caesar." This binary structure makes for a very quick-paced movie that emphasizes the main events in the play. In his focus on the lynching of Cinna the Poet and his use of chiaroscuro effects, Bradley might have been influenced by the 1937 stage production directed by Orson Welles. The film's aesthetic is based on a contrast between darkness and sudden flashes of light, on some extreme close-ups and on pronounced high- or low-angle shots. The characters are thus often turned into spectral figures coming out of German expressionistic films. Bradley also uses editing techniques directly inspired by the Russian director, Sergei Eisenstein, to create visual metaphors. The production made full use of its Chicago locations, notably the steps of the downtown post office and the portico of the Elks' national headquarters, which helped to create the look of a Greco-Roman city. Due to budget restraints, students were recruited from Northwestern University to work as extras, and because only one horse could be hired per day for the battle scenes, the footage had to be cleverly edited to create more or less realistic impressions. The orchestra which performed the film score consisted of only nine brass instruments, and was recorded in an out-of-use indoor swimming pool to create echo and a larger sound. Bradley's film is famous for including one of Charlton Heston's first screen performances. Heston was again to play Mark Antony in Stuart Burge's film twenty years later.

In the 1953 black-and-white Hollywood production, director Joseph L. Mankiewicz concentrates on the sheer size of the events and combines the style of American actors (Marlon Brando as Antony, Louis Calhern as Caesar) with that of British actors (John Gielgud as Cassius and James Mason as Brutus). The medium of cinema allows the impressive crowd sequences to be made, importing the familiar aesthetic of the Hollywood epic and recycling the codes of Roman films such as the 1951 *Quo Vadis* (the sets of which were actually used again for this film). The original music, composed by Miklos Rozsa, crucially irrigates the film, giving it monumental power and unity through recurrent musical themes. The shifts in authority between the characters are made ostensible through changes in camera angles, but some dialogue scenes are closer to a stage approach. The camera is sometimes motionless and the number of different shots is reduced. Mankiewicz, fearing to disrupt the fluidity and the emotional breadth of scenes, frequently films the actors' confrontation, as well as their monologues, within the same shot. The two women (Portia and Calphurnia) are given prominence as they attempt with all their might to convince their husbands either to confide a secret or avoid danger. But the main visual focus of this *Julius Caesar* is Caesar's imperial omnipresence in the form of statues or eagles that invade almost every set of the film, including the credits. Made in post-war America, this production puts the stress on the corruption and tyranny at work in Fascist regimes. Marlon Brando has been praised for his Machiavellian performance of Antony as an opportunistic and manipulative orator. The film does not glorify the conspirators eithers, but presents them with all their jealousy, weakness and pettiness. The film not only draws from Shakespeare's playscript but also from Shakespeare's sources, as two intertitles (one at the very start and one before the Proscription scene) are inspired by Plutarch's *Lives* and provide the audience with some historical context and date.

The 1970 film, directed in a widescreen format by Stuart Burge and shot in Technicolor, offers a new epic take on the play. At the release of the film, the tagline was "No grander Caesar... No greater cast!" Most of the film promotion was indeed based on the all-star cast—Charlton Heston (again appearing as Antony), Richard Chamberlain (as Octavius), John Gielgud (playing Caesar after having played Cassius in the Mankiewicz film), Diana Rigg (as Portia), Jason Robards (as Brutus), etc. The film, however, failed with the critics who often condemned Robards's cold and stiff performance as Brutus. But the film does contain some striking cinematic moments at times, notably in its imaginative use of flashback and flashforward to construct Calphurnia's dream, in its stress on the gory aspects of Caesar's assassination and in its staging of a full-blown, highly realistic battle at Philippi.

The BBC-TV *Julius Caesar*, directed by Herbert Wise and produced by Cedric Messina, was recorded between 26 and 31 July 1978, only cutting a few lines from the play. The settings standing for Rome are far from realistic—the streets feature no passers-by and no shops. The show focuses entirely on the characters in the play without offering any distraction. However, the battle sequences adopt a more naturalistic look with extras for the fighting and an exterior-looking landscape. Soliloquies are both voiced over and spoken, which creates the impression that the characters are having a discussion with themselves. The voice-over also allows the characters to speak much more rapidly, giving the natural sense of thinking rather than delivering their lines. The visual motif of this production is blood: Caesar's murder ends in a pool of blood in which the conspirators immerse not only their hands but their arms up to the elbows. Brutus's oration thus starts with the raising of his hands splattered with Caesar's blood. It is also only in this film that Portia's bleeding wound in the thigh is fully revealed.

Whether filmed for the cinema or television, the four screen versions using Shakespeare's text all present a very complex world where the notions of good and evil are blurred. No film constructs one specific hero or revels in the victory of the Triumvirate's side. All the directors let the spectators decide for themselves the lessons to be drawn from this rewriting of Roman history.

Sarah Hatchuel, 2007

**Editor's Note:** In this edition, I have tried to preserve Kittredge's voice as much as possible while updating his notes. I have deleted many long quotations from North's translation of Plutarch and some passages in which I felt Kittredge acted less as an editor and more as a director, informing us of the gestures, moves and thoughts of the characters at particular moments. I chose to suppress those details to preserve the reader's own personal interpretation of each scene. My priority, for this edition, was the reader's understanding of the text itself. Therefore, I have added explanations for some words and ideas on which Kittredge felt he did not need to comment as he often assumed knowledge among his readers of historical or mythic figures that is no longer common. I also inserted some more detailed notes comparing several film performances of *Julius Caesar*. I hope that the updates and additions will enrich the experience of reading and studying the play. All the added notes are followed by [S.H.] to distinguish them from Kittredge's original work.

[S.H.]

# THE TRAGEDY OF
# JULIUS CAESAR

## Dramatis Personæ

Julius Caesar.

Octavius Caesar, ⎫ Triumvirs after the
Marcus Antonius, ⎬ death of *Julius Caesar*.
Lepidus, ⎭

Cicero, ⎫
Publius, ⎬ Senators.
Popilius Lena, ⎭

Marcus Brutus ⎫
Cassius, ⎪
Casca, ⎪
Trebonius, ⎪ Conspirators
Ligarius, ⎬ against
Decius Brutus, ⎪ *Julius Caesar*.
Metellus Cimber, ⎪
Cinna, ⎭

Flavius and *Marullus*, Tribunes of the
    People.
Artemidorus, a teacher of rhetoric.
A Soothsayer.
Cinna, a poet.
Another Poet.

Lucilius, ⎫
Titinius, ⎪
Messala, ⎬ friends to *Brutus*
Young Cato, ⎪ and *Cassius*.
Volumnius, ⎭

Varro, ⎫
Clitus, ⎪
Claudius, ⎬ servants to *Brutus*.
Strato, ⎪
Lucius, ⎪
Dardanius, ⎭

Pindarus, servant to *Cassius*.
A Servant to *Caesar*; to *Antony*; to
    *Octavius*.

Calphurnia, wife to *Caesar*.
Portia, wife to *Brutus*.

The Ghost of *Caesar*.

Senators, Citizens, Guards, Attendants.

SCENE.—*Rome; near Sardis; near Philippi.*

# ACT I

### SCENE I. [*Rome. A street.*]

*Enter* Flavius, Marullus, *and certain* Commoners *over the stage.*

FLAV.   Hence! Home, you idle creatures, get you home!†
        Is this a holiday? What, know you not,
        Being mechanical, you ought not walk
        Upon a labouring day without the sign
        Of your profession? Speak, what trade art thou?          5

CARPENTER   Why, sir, a carpenter.

MAR.    Where is thy leather apron and thy rule?
        What dost thou with thy best apparel on?
        You, sir, what trade are you?

COBBLER   Truly, sir, in respect of a fine workman I am but, as you would say, a
        cobbler.                                                 11

MAR.    But what trade art thou? Answer me directly.

COB.    A trade, sir, that I hope I may use with a safe conscience, which is indeed,
        sir, a mender of bad soles.

MAR.    What trade, thou knave? Thou naughty knave, what trade?    15

---

ACT I. SCENE I.

Flavius and Marullus, as Tribunes of the People, are leaders of the popular or democratic party and therefore opposed to Caesar's ambitious plans. **Over the stage** is a conventional phrase indicating that the actors enter and cross the stage before they come to a halt. 3. **Being mechanical:** belonging to the working class, having a trade. 4. **sign:** for example, work clothes and tools. [S.H.] 5. **profession:** trade, occupation.— **thou:** An old distinction between the pronouns *thou* and *you* was preserved in Elizabethan English. *Thou* was the more familiar form of address. 7. **rule:** tool for measurement, with a pun on controlled behaviour. [S.H.] 10. **in respect of:** in comparison with. 11. **a cobbler:** a botcher, an unskilled or clumsy workman (in antithesis to "fine workman"). The word meant also "a repairer of shoes," and this is in fact the speaker's trade; but he resorts to ambiguity in order to mislead Marullus, who understands him in the general sense (botcher) and therefore repeats his question with emphasis: "But what *trade* art thou? Answer me directly" (straightforwardly, without evasion or quibbling). 14. **soles:** The play on *sole* and *soul* was one of the commonest of puns. 15. **naughty:** rascally.

---

† In Bradley's 1950 film, the people wishing to attend Caesar's triumph are seen eating and shouting in close-ups. The Tribune's oration against their cheering anticipates Antony's speech in the Forum scene as he is filmed in a low-angle shot up the Senate stairs, highlighting his powerful rhetoric. As the second Tribune destroys bunches of flowers, scattering every petal on the ground, the film creates a metaphor foreshadowing the fall of Caesar. Mankiewicz's 1953 version opens on Caesar's bust decorated with flowers while a busy crowd is cheering in the background. The first Tribune violently removes the flowers from the statue and throws them to the ground, but he is immediately arrested by a soldier. Mankiewicz's opening thus presents a military and dictatorial state, based on the cult of Caesar's personality. [S.H.]

COB.    Nay, I beseech you, sir, be not out with me. Yet if you be out, sir, I can mend you.

MAR.    What mean'st thou by that? Mend me, thou saucy fellow?

COB.    Why, sir, cobble you.

FLAV.    Thou art a cobbler, art thou?     20

COB.    Truly, sir, all that I live by is with the awl. I meddle with no tradesman's matters nor women's matters, but with all. I am indeed, sir, a surgeon to old shoes. When they are in great danger, I recover them. As proper men as ever trod upon neat's leather have gone upon my handiwork.

FLAV.    But wherefore art not in thy shop today?     25
Why dost thou lead these men about the streets?

COB.    Truly, sir, to wear out their shoes, to get myself into more work. But indeed, sir, we make holiday to see Caesar and to rejoice in his triumph.

MAR.    Wherefore rejoice? What conquest brings he home?
What tributaries follow him to Rome     30
To grace in captive bonds his chariot wheels?
You blocks, you stones, you worse than senseless things!
O you hard hearts, you cruel men of Rome!
Knew you not Pompey? Many a time and oft
Have you climb'd up to walls and battlements,     35
To tow'rs and windows, yea, to chimney tops,
Your infants in your arms, and there have sat
The livelong day, with patient expectation,
To see great Pompey pass the streets of Rome.
And when you saw his chariot but appear,     40
Have you not made an universal shout,
That Tiber trembled underneath her banks
To hear the replication of your sounds
Made in her concave shores?

---

16. **out with me:** out of temper with me, offended with me. 17. **mend you:** pun on "mend your shoes" and "set you right." [S.H.] 19. **cobble you:** mend your shoes. 21. **all...awl:** proverbial, with a sexual pun on the cobbler's awl, a pointed hand tool with a fluted blade used for piercing leather or wood. [S.H.]— **meddle:** mix, with sexual innuendo. [S.H.] 22. **with all. I am:** The cobbler continues his punning: "with *all* matters," "with everything," and "with awl."— **indeed:** in very truth, to speak seriously. 23. **recover:** The pun is obvious. *Recover* in the sense of "cure," "save," was common.—**proper:** handsome. 24. **neat's leather:** cowhide [S.H.]—**gone:** walked. 28. **triumph:** victory, triumphal procession. [S.H.] 29. **What conquest brings he home?** Caesar's triumph was not for conquest (spoils of war [S.H.]) of a foreign foe but for victory in a civil war against Pompey. 30. **tributaries:** captives who must pay tribute [S.H.] 31. **To grace:** to do honor to. 34. **Pompey:** Pompey the Great (B.C. 106-48) formed the first triumvirate with Caesar and Crassus. An outstanding commander and son-in-law of Caesar, he ultimately became Caesar's rival and was defeated at Pharsalus. He fled to Egypt and was murdered there. [S.H.] 42. **That:** so that.— **her banks:** Rivers are sometimes personified as masculine and sometimes as feminine. The Tiber is usually spoken of as Father Tiber. 43. **replication:** reverberation. 44. **concave:** scooped out, curved. [S.H.]

|  | And do you now put on your best attire? | 45 |
|  | And do you now cull out a holiday? |  |
|  | And do you now strew flowers in his way |  |
|  | That comes in triumph over Pompey's blood? |  |
|  | Be gone! |  |
|  | Run to your houses, fall upon your knees, | 50 |
|  | Pray to the gods to intermit the plague |  |
|  | That needs must light on this ingratitude. |  |

FLAV.      Go, go, good countrymen, and for this fault
          Assemble all the poor men of your sort;
          Draw them to Tiber banks, and weep your tears     55
          Into the channel, till the lowest stream
          Do kiss the most exalted shores of all.

                                          *Exeunt all the Commoners.*

          See, whe'r their basest mettle be not mov'd.
          They vanish tongue-tied in their guiltiness.
          Go you down that way towards the Capitol;       60
          This way will I. Disrobe the images
          If you do find them deck'd with ceremonies.

MAR.      May we do so?
          You know it is the feast of Lupercal.

FLAV.      It is no matter. Let no images                 65
          Be hung with Caesar's trophies. I'll about
          And drive away the vulgar from the streets.
          So do you too, where you perceive them thick.
          These growing feathers pluck'd from Caesar's wing
          Will make him fly an ordinary pitch,          70

---

46. **cull out a holiday:** select one out of the working days of the week and make a holiday of it. 48. **Pompey's blood:** Pompey's kin. The victory was the Battle of Munda, in Spain, in which Pompey's two sons were defeated by Caesar on March 17, B.C., 45. The triumph was celebrated in October, B.C. 45. Shakespeare puts it on the day of the next Lupercalia—which was, in fact, February 15, B.C. 44. 51. **intermit:** suspend, postpone. The punishment must come sooner or later, but the citizens are to pray that it may be long deferred. 53. **Go, go:** Flavius adopts a more conciliatory tone than his colleague. 54. **sort:** rank, class. 56-57. **till the lowest…all:** so that the stream, even if it is now at its lowest, may rise to the highest point it ever reaches, even in times of flood. The inundations of the Tiber have been proverbial for two thousand years. 58. **whe'r:** a contraction of *whether.*—**mettle:** nature, temper, disposition. 62. **ceremonies:** ornaments indicating a religious celebration; here, triumphal ornaments. The Roman triumph was essentially a religious ceremony. The reference is to the "scarfs" with which Caesar's images are decked. 64. **feast of Lupercal:** the festival of the Lupercalia, celebrated in February in honor of the Italian god Lupercus, worshipped as the protector of flocks against wolves and as a patron of agriculture. To disrobe the images was to disturb the peace at this time of religious observance. Besides, the "scarfs," though really in honor of Caesar, might also be regarded as decorations for the Lupercalia. On both grounds the action urged by Marullus would be sacrilegious. 66. **I'll about:** I'll go about. The ellipsis of the verb of motion is common in such phrases. 67. **vulgar:** the common people, the plebeians. 68. **thick:** dense. [S.H.] 70. **pitch:** height. A term of falconry, meaning the highest point attained by a soaring hawk.

Who else would soar above the view of men
And keep us all in servile fearfulness.                    *Exeunt.*

## SCENE II. [*Rome. A public place.*]

[*Music.*] *Enter* Caesar, Antony (*for the course*), Calphurnia, Portia, Decius, Cicero,
Brutus, Cassius, Casca, [*a great crowd following, among them, a* Soothsayer; *after
them,* Marullus *and* Flavius].

| | | |
|---|---|---|
| CAES. | Calphurnia.† | |
| CASCA | Peace, ho! Caesar speaks. | [*Music ceases.*] |
| CAES. | Calphurnia. | |
| CAL. | Here, my lord. | |
| CAES. | Stand you directly in Antonius' way | |
| | When he doth run his course. Antonius. | |

CAES.    Stand you directly in Antonius' way
When he doth run his course. Antonius.

ANT.    Caesar, my lord?                                    5

CAES.    Forget not in your speed, Antonius,
To touch Calphurnia; for our elders say
The barren, touched in this holy chase,
Shake off their sterile curse.‡

ANT.                                    I shall remember.
When Caesar says 'Do this,' it is perform'd.                10

CAES.    Set on, and leave no ceremony out.                [*Music.*]

SOOTH.    Caesar!

CAES.    Ha! Who calls?

CASCA    Bid every noise be still. Peace yet again!        [*Music ceases.*]

---

71. **above the view of men:** out of the sight of men, i.e., would become a god.

**SCENE II.**

This scene takes place on the same day as scene 1. Mark Antony enters stripped **"for the course":** he is dressed for the Lupercalia ceremony in which young men, clad only in a girdle round the loins, run a race through the streets, striking any they met with leather strips. [S.H.] 4. **run his course:** in the race which formed a part of the celebration of the Lupercalia. 9. **sterile curse:** curse of barrenness. 11. **Set on:** move on.

---

†    In Bradley's 1950 film, Caesar first appears alone with the victorious laurel crown on his head, filmed in a majestic low-angle shot. By contrast, Mankiewicz's 1953 epic production features a spectacular procession seen from afar and involving hundreds of extras celebrating Caesar's triumph. The 1970 film by Burge presents the procession at a much closer range. The camera remains rather fixed while chariots, performers and revelers march past. [S.H.]

‡    Note Calphurnia's upset but dignified reaction at Caesar's order to Antony in Mankiewicz's film. [S.H.]

Caesar's triumph in Mankiewicz's 1953 epic film (1.2.1).

| | | |
|---|---|---|
| CAES. | Who is it in the press that calls on me? | 15 |
| | I hear a tongue shriller than all the music | |
| | Cry 'Caesar!' Speak. Caesar is turn'd to hear. | |
| SOOTH. | Beware the ides of March. | |
| CAES. | What man is that? | |
| BRU. | A soothsayer bids you beware the ides of March. | |
| CAES. | Set him before me; let me see his face. | 20 |
| CASS. | Fellow, come from the throng; look upon Caesar. | |
| CAES. | What say'st thou to me now? Speak once again. | |
| SOOTH. | Beware the ides of March.† | |

---

15. **press:** crowd. 18. **the ides of March:** the fifteenth of the month. [S.H.]

†    Bradley's 1950 film starts with this sentence, thus emphasizing the prophesy's importance. The Soothsayer's face appears out of the shadow and comes to the fore progressively, until it invades the whole screen. The film then cuts directly to the title "Julius Caesar" written in Roman style, while an ominous and dramatic music can be heard. It is as though the Soothsayer himself was giving birth to the entire film. Later on, he reappears before Caesar in the form of a black, cloaked, death-like figure. In Mankiewicz's 1953 version, the Soothsayer is blind and is left behind while Caesar and the whole procession move away. The film thus stresses the lethal mistake of not paying attention to the prophecy. The Soothsayer then gropes for physical contact and, as he explores Brutus's face, he suddenly gives a start, as if he knew that this man was to become Caesar's future murderer. [S.H.]

CAES.   He is a dreamer. Let us leave him.
        Pass.

                        *Sennet. Exeunt. All but* Brutus *and* Cassius.

CASS.   Will you go see the order of the course?                        25

BRU.    Not I.

CASS.   I pray you do.

BRU.    I am not gamesome. I do lack some part
        Of that quick spirit that is in Antony.
        Let me not hinder, Cassius, your desires.                       30
        I'll leave you.

CASS.   Brutus, I do observe you now of late;
        I have not from your eyes that gentleness
        And show of love as I was wont to have.
        You bear too stubborn and too strange a hand                    35
        Over your friend that loves you.

BRU.                            Cassius,
        Be not deceiv'd. If I have veil'd my look,
        I turn the trouble of my countenance
        Merely upon myself. Vexed I am
        Of late with passions of some difference,                       40
        Conceptions only proper to myself,
        Which give some soil, perhaps, to my behaviours;
        But let not therefore my good friends be griev'd
        (Among which number, Cassius, be you one)
        Nor construe any further my neglect                             45
        Than that poor Brutus, with himself at war,†
        Forgets the shows of love to other men.

---

24. **Pass:** pass on, go forward.—**Sennet:** trumpet signal. 25. **the order of the course:** the proceedings at the race. 29. **quick spirit:** liveliness. 34. **show:** appearance.—**as:** that.—**wont:** accustomed [S.H.] 35. **You bear…hand:** You treat your friend too roughly and too much like a stranger. The figure is from riding or driving a horse.—**stubborn:** rough, harsh. 37–39. **If…myself:** If my looks have been less open and friendly, the troubled expression of my face is altogether due to personal matters (not to unfriendliness toward you).—**merely:** entirely, altogether. 40. **passions of some difference:** strong and conflicting emotions. 41. **only proper to myself:** concerning myself alone. 42. **soil:** smirch, stain. 43. **griev'd:** aggrieved, offended. 44. **be you one:** count yourself one, continue to be my friend. 45-46. **construe…Than:** interpret my neglect as meaning anything more than, etc.

---

†    Brutus's inner division and burdensome dilemma are often shown in visual terms. Bradley's film emphasizes the shadow that Brutus projects on the wall, thus creating a double vision of the character. Brutus's face is also divided with chiaroscuro lighting: one side is lit while the other remains in the dark. His quandary is made visually explicit when the camera films Brutus behind a gate, figuratively trapping him in a net of troubles. [S.H.]

| Cass. | Then, Brutus, I have much mistook your passion; |
| | By means whereof this breast of mine hath buried |
| | Thoughts of great value, worthy cogitations. | 50 |
| | Tell me, good Brutus, can you see your face? |

| Bru. | No, Cassius; for the eye sees not itself |
| | But by reflection, by some other things. |

| Cass. | 'Tis just. |
| | And it is very much lamented, Brutus, | 55 |
| | That you have no such mirrors as will turn |
| | Your hidden worthiness into your eye, |
| | That you might see your shadow. I have heard |
| | Where many of the best respect in Rome |
| | (Except immortal Caesar), speaking of Brutus | 60 |
| | And groaning underneath this age's yoke, |
| | Have wish'd that noble Brutus had his eyes. |

| Bru. | Into what dangers would you lead me, Cassius, |
| | That you would have me seek into myself |
| | For that which is not in me? | 65 |

| Cass. | Therefore, good Brutus, be prepar'd to hear; |
| | And since you know you cannot see yourself |
| | So well as by reflection, I, your glass, |
| | Will modestly discover to yourself |
| | That of yourself which you yet know not of. | 70 |
| | And be not jealous on me, gentle Brutus. |
| | Were I a common laugher, or did use |
| | To stale with ordinary oaths my love |
| | To every new protester; if you know |
| | That I do fawn on men and hug them hard, | 75 |
| | And after scandal them; or if you know |
| | That I profess myself in banqueting |
| | To all the rout, then hold me dangerous. |

*Flourish and shout.*

---

48. **mistook your passion:** misinterpreted your troubled feelings. 49-50. **By means whereof...worthy cogitations:** Because of this, I have kept some thoughts to myself. [S.H.] 53. **But by reflection, by some other things:** except by reflection, by means of some other things (such as a mirror or any polished surface). 54. **just:** true, exactly. so. 56. **turn:** reflect. 57. **Your hidden worthiness:** your great and noble qualities, of which you are unconscious. 58. **shadow:** image in a mirror. 59. **of the best respect:** of the best repute, most highly regarded. 62. **had his eyes:** "would see how things stand" or "saw things as any anti-Caesarian does." [S.H.] 68. **glass:** mirror. [S.H.] 69. **modestly:** moderately (without exaggeration), like a faithful mirror.—**discover:** disclose, reveal. 71. **jealous on me:** suspicious of me. 72. **common laughter:** subject of jest. [S.H.] 74. **protester:** one who strongly professes friendship. 75. **fawn:** flatter, seek attention by making oneself agreeable [S.H.] 76. **scandal:** slander. 77. **profess myself:** make emphatic professions of friendship. 78. **rout:** crowd.

BRU.           What means this shouting? I do fear the people
                    Choose Caesar for their king.

CASS.                               Ay, do you fear it?          80
                    Then must I think you would not have it so.

BRU.           I would not, Cassius; yet I love him well.
                    But wherefore do you hold me here so long?
                    What is it that you would impart to me?
                    If it be aught toward the general good,          85
                    Set honor in one eye and death i' th' other,
                    And I will look on both indifferently;
                    For let the gods so speed me as I love
                    The name of honor more than I fear death.

CASS.          I know that virtue to be in you, Brutus,         90
                    As well as I do know your outward favor.
                    Well, honor is the subject of my story.
                    I cannot tell what you and other men
                    Think of this life; but for my single self,
                    I had as lief not be as live to be           95
                    In awe of such a thing as I myself.
                    I was born free as Caesar; so were you.
                    We both have fed as well, and we can both
                    Endure the winter's cold as well as he.
                    For once, upon a raw and gusty day,†       100
                    The troubled Tiber chafing with her shores,
                    Caesar said to me, 'Dar'st thou, Cassius, now
                    Leap in with me into this angry flood
                    And swim to yonder point?' Upon the word,
                    Accoutred as I was, I plunged in          105
                    And bade him follow. So indeed he did.

---

80. **Choose Caesar for their king:** The worst fear of Brutus is that Caesar will usurp royal authority. This anxiety betrays itself in an unguarded exclamation, which gives Cassius precisely the opening he desires. 85. **aught:** anything. [S.H.] 86–89. **Set honor...death:** set both death and honor before my eyes—**speed me:** prosper me, show me favor. 90. **that virtue:** the manly virtue of preferring honor to everything else—even to life. 91. **your outward favor:** the features of your face. 95. **lief:** soon. [S.H.] 101. **chafing with her shores:** quarreling with her shores, dashing against her banks as if in anger. 105. **accoutred:** dressed or armed. [S.H.]

---

†    In Bradley's 1950 film, this part of Cassius's speech is transformed into a flashback showing the events that are only narrated in Shakespeare's text. The images show Caesar and Cassius swimming, then Caesar starting to drown and being helped by Cassius. This visual insert puts the stress on Caesar's weakness, before cutting back to Cassius's face. In this version, Cassius is almost made monstrous with extreme close-ups on his gaunt face, his eyes and his teeth. This underlines his power of conviction but also his ability to hurt his enemies. In Mankiewicz's 1953 production, by contrast, no images come to illustrate Cassius's speech. But Caesar looms over the place in the form of numerous statues. [S.H.]

"And this man is now become a god" (1.2.115): Cassius near Caesar's statue in Mankiewicz's 1953 film.

The torrent roar'd, and we did buffet it
With lusty sinews, throwing it aside
And stemming it with hearts of controversy.
But ere we could arrive the point propos'd,                                    110
Caesar cried, 'Help me, Cassius, or I sink!'
I, as Aeneas, our great ancestor,
Did from the flames of Troy upon his shoulder
The old Anchises bear, so from the waves of Tiber
Did I the tired Caesar. And this man                                           115
Is now become a god,† and Cassius is
A wretched creature and must bend his body
If Caesar carelessly but nod on him.
He had a fever when he was in Spain,
And when the fit was on him, I did mark                                         120
How he did shake. 'Tis true, this god did shake.

---

106. **bade:** bid. [S.H.] 107. **buffet:** beat. [S.H.] 109. **stemming:** breasting, pushing through. [S.H.]—
**hearts of controversy:** hearts of eager rivalry. 110. **ere:** before [S.H.] —**arrive:** arrive at. 112. **Aeneas…
Anchises bear:** In Virgil's *Aeneid*, the Trojan hero Aeneas rescues his father, Anchises, from Troy as the
Greeks burn it. Aeneas later founded Rome. [S.H.] 120. **the fit:** the ague fit, the chill.

---

†        In Bradley's film, this line is visually illustrated by a shot of an all-powerful Caesar filmed from below
         while he is nodding conceitedly at a subject. Mankiewicz's version chooses a more metaphorical way
         of expressing Cassius's grievance. Cassius is filmed with a high-angle shot, below a bust of Caesar
         looking down upon him like a deity. [S.H.]

His coward lips did from their color fly,
And that same eye whose bend doth awe the world
Did lose his lustre. I did hear him groan.
Ay, and that tongue of his that bade the Romans                    125
Mark him and write his speeches in their books,
Alas, it cried, 'Give me some drink, Titinius,'
As a sick girl! Ye gods, it doth amaze me
A man of such a feeble temper should
So get the start of the majestic world                             130
And bear the palm alone.

                                        *Shout. Flourish.*

BRU.      Another general shout?
I do believe that these applauses are
For some new honours that are heap'd on Caesar.

CASS.     Why, man, he doth bestride the narrow world                 135
Like a Colossus, and we petty men
Walk under his huge legs and peep about
To find ourselves dishonorable graves.
Men at some time are masters of their fates.
The fault, dear Brutus, is not in our stars,                       140
But in ourselves, that we are underlings.
'Brutus,' and 'Caesar.' What should be in that 'Caesar'?
Why should that name be sounded more than yours?
Write them together: yours is as fair a name.†
Sound them: it doth become the mouth as well.                      145
Weigh them: it is as heavy. Conjure with 'em:
'Brutus' will start a spirit as soon as 'Caesar.'
Now in the names of all the gods at once,

---

122. **His coward lips,** etc. The lips are said to have *abandoned their color(s)* like cowardly soldiers. The pun would be impossible in modern English, which no longer uses *color* (singular) in the sense of "flag." 123. **bend:** look, glance. 124. **his:** its. 128. **amaze me:** reduce me to a state of utter stupefaction, not merely "surprise me." 129. **temper:** physical temperament. 130-131. **get the start...world,** etc. Caesar has outstripped the whole world in the race for power.—**the palm:** the prize of victory. 135. **bestride:** straddle. [S.H.] 136. **Colossus:** a gigantic statue. [S.H.] 140. **our stars:** the stars that rule our lives. 141. **underlings:** persons of low birth. [S.H.] 143. **be sounded more:** be more celebrated in men's talk. 145. **doth become:** it befits, it suits. [S.H.] 146. **Conjure with 'em:** Use them as formulae of conjuration. It was thought that certain names and certain forms of words were powerful in calling up spirits and subjecting them to the control of the conjurer.—**'em:** a clipped form of *hem*—a Middle English form of *he*.

---

†    At this moment, in Burge's 1970 screen version, Cassius takes a knife and, on the wall, carves the name "Brutus" beneath already-made *graffiti* of Caesar's name. The sharp cutting of the wall combined with the brick red color of the newly-carved name anticipates Caesar's assassination. This is made even more obvious when Cassius soon scratches off Caesar's name with a resentful stroke of his knife. A link is made between the name and the person, between the words and the future deed. [S.H.]

Upon what meat doth this our Caesar feed
That he is grown so great? Age, thou art sham'd!                    150
Rome, thou hast lost the breed of noble bloods!
When went there by an age since the great Flood
But it was fam'd with more than with one man?
When could they say (till now) that talk'd of Rome
That her wide walls encompass'd but one man?                        155
Now is it Rome indeed, and room enough,
When there is in it but one only man!
O, you and I have heard our fathers say
There was a Brutus once that would have brook'd
Th' eternal devil to keep his state in Rome                         160
As easily as a king.†

BRU.    That you do love me I am nothing jealous.
What you would work me to, I have some aim.
How I have thought of this, and of these times,
I shall recount hereafter. For this present,                        165
I would not (so with love I might entreat you)
Be any further mov'd. What you have said
I will consider; what you have to say
I will with patience hear, and find a time
Both meet to hear and answer such high things.                      170
Till then, my noble friend, chew upon this:
Brutus had rather be a villager
Than to repute himself a son of Rome
Under these hard conditions as this time
Is like to lay upon us.

---

151. **thou hast lost...bloods:** thy nobles are all degenerate.—**noble bloods:** persons of noble birth and noble nature. 152. **great Flood:** In Greek mythology, Zeus drowns all mankind for wickedness, save Deucalion and his wife Pyrrha, spared for their virtues. [S.H.] 153. **fam'd with:** made famous by, celebrated for. 156. **Rome...room enough:** This pun on *Rome* and *room* was common. The words were pronounced alike or nearly alike. 159. **There was a Brutus once:** About B.C. 509, Lucius Junius Brutus ousted the tyrant Tarquinius and became first Consul. Marcus Brutus claimed descent from him. [S.H.]—**brook'd:** suffered, endured, allowed. 160-161. **Th' eternal devil...king:** would have been as ready to give Rome over to the rule of the devil forever as to allow a king to set up his throne there.—**keep his state:** set up and maintain royal authority. 162. **nothing jealous:** not at all doubtful. 163. **aim:** guess. 165. **For this present:** at the present moment. 166. **so...you:** if I might be allowed to ask it of you as a friend. 167. **mov'd:** urged, prompted. 170. **meet:** fitting. [S.H.] 171. **chew upon:** ponder. 173. **repute:** esteem. [S.H.] 174. **as:** which. 175. **like:** likely.

---

†    At this point, in Mankiewicz's 1953 film, Cassius turns toward a statue that we understand to be one of Junius Brutus, Brutus's own ancestor. The presence of statues in this scene stresses the overwhelming presence of Caesar but also that of Rome's glorious figures of the past. This move is part of Cassius's strategy to put pressure on Brutus and convince him to join the conspiracy. In the BBC 1979 production, Brutus stares wide-eyed at the mention of his famous ancestor, only to lower his gaze immediately after, as if in shame. [S.H.]

| Cass. | I am glad | 175 |
| | That my weak words have struck but thus much show | |
| | Of fire from Brutus. | |

*Enter* Caesar *and his* Train.

| Bru. | The games are done, and Caesar is returning. | |
| Cass. | As they pass by, pluck Casca by the sleeve, | |
| | And he will (after his sour fashion) tell you | 180 |
| | What hath proceeded worthy note today. | |
| Bru. | I will do so. But look you, Cassius! | |
| | The angry spot doth glow on Caesar's brow, | |
| | And all the rest look like a chidden train. | |
| | Calphurnia's cheek is pale, and Cicero | 185 |
| | Looks with such ferret and such fiery eyes | |
| | As we have seen him in the Capitol, | |
| | Being cross'd in conference by some senators. | |
| Cass. | Casca will tell us what the matter is. | |
| Caes. | Antonius. | 190 |
| Ant. | Caesar? | |
| Caes. | Let me have men about me that are fat, | |
| | Sleek-headed men, and such as sleep a-nights. | |
| | Yond Cassius has a lean and hungry look. | |
| | He thinks too much. Such men are dangerous. | 195 |
| Ant. | Fear him not, Caesar; he's not dangerous. | |
| | He is a noble Roman, and well given. | |
| Caes. | Would he were fatter! But I fear him not. | |
| | Yet if my name were liable to fear, | |
| | I do not know the man I should avoid | 200 |
| | So soon as that spare Cassius. He reads much, | |
| | He is a great observer, and he looks | |
| | Quite through the deeds of men. He loves no plays | |
| | As thou dost, Antony; he hears no music. | |
| | Seldom he smiles, and smiles in such a sort | 205 |
| | As if he mock'd himself and scorn'd his spirit | |

---

178. **games:** the "course" mentioned in 1.2.25. 181. **proceeded:** gone on, taken place.—**worthy note:** noteworthy. [S.H.] 184. **chidden:** scolded. [S.H.] 186–188. **ferret:** bloodshot (from angry excitement). The ferret has small red eyes.—**conference:** debate. 193. **sleek-headed:** unworried. [S.H.] —**a-nights:** of nights. 194. **Yond:** yonder. Hardly distinguishable in meaning from an emphatic *that.* 197. **well given:** well-disposed. 199. **if my name were liable to fear:** a formal way of saying, "If Caesar were liable to fear." The suggestion is that the name *Caesar* and the word *fear* are incompatible terms. 205. **in such a sort:** in such a way.

That could be mov'd to smile at anything.
Such men as he be never at heart's ease
Whiles they behold a greater than themselves,
And therefore are they very dangerous.                          210
I rather tell thee what is to be fear'd
Than what I fear; for always I am Caesar.
Come on my right hand, for this ear is deaf,
And tell me truly what thou think'st of him.

          *Sennet. Exeunt* Caesar *and his* Train.    [*Except* Casca.]

CASCA   You pull'd me by the cloak. Would you speak with me?        215

BRU.    Ay, Casca. Tell us what hath chanc'd today
        That Caesar looks so sad.

CASCA   Why, you were with him, were you not?

BRU.    I should not then ask Casca what had chanc'd.

CASCA   Why, there was a crown offer'd him; and being offer'd him, he put it by
        with the back of his hand thus; and then the people fell a-shouting.

BRU.    What was the second noise for?                              222

CASCA   Why, for that too.†

CASS.   They shouted thrice. What was the last cry for?

CASCA   Why, for that too.                                          225

BRU.    Was the crown offer'd him thrice?

CASCA   Ay, marry, was't! and he put it by thrice, every time gentler than other;
        and at every putting-by mine honest neighbours shouted.

CASS.   Who offer'd him the crown?

CASCA   Why, Antony.                                                230

BRU.    Tell us the manner of it, gentle Casca.

CASCA   I can as well be hang'd as tell the manner of it. It was mere foolery; I
        did not mark it. I saw Mark Antony offer him a crown—yet 'twas not a
        crown neither, 'twas one of these coronets—and, as I told you, he put it

---

209. **Whiles:** while, so long as. 212. **always I am Caesar:** and that name *Caesar,* as he has just proudly asserted, is not "liable to fear" (1.2.199). 213. **this ear is deaf:** This graphic touch is Shakespeare's own. There is no ancient authority for Caesar's deafness. 215. **You pull'd me by the cloak:** Casca speaks in prose, and in an abrupt, impatient style according well with "his sour fashion" (1.2.180). 216. **chanc'd:** occurred. [S.H.] 232. **mere:** pure, downright. 234. **coronets:** A coronet ("little crown") is a crown of an inferior sort appropriated not to kings but to dukes.

---

†    In the BBC 1979 version, Casca is played as a direct, cynical and detached man, slightly annoyed at
     Brutus and Cassius's queries, and giving very bored and repetitive answers. [S.H.]

by once; but for all that, to my thinking, he would fain have had it. Then he offered it to him again; then he put it by again; but to my thinking, he was very loath to lay his fingers off it. And then he offered it the third time. He put it the third time by; and still as he refus'd it, the rabblement hooted, and clapp'd their chopt hands, and threw up their sweaty night-caps, and uttered such a deal of stinking breath because Caesar refus'd the crown that it had, almost, chok'd Caesar; for he swoonded and fell down at it. And for mine own part, I durst not laugh, for fear of opening my lips and receiving the bad air.† 243

CASS.   But soft, I pray you. What, did Caesar swound?

CASCA   He fell down in the market place and foam'd at mouth and was speechless. 246

BRU.   'Tis very like. He hath the falling sickness.

CASS.   No, Caesar hath it not; but you, and I,
And honest Casca, we have the falling sickness.

CASCA   I know not what you mean by that, but I am sure Caesar fell down. If the tag-rag people did not clap him and hiss him, according as he pleas'd and displeas'd them, as they use to do the players in the theatre, I am no true man. 253

BRU.   What said he when he came unto himself?

CASCA   Marry, before he fell down, when he perceiv'd the common herd was glad he refus'd the crown, he pluck'd me ope his doublet and offer'd them his throat to cut. An I had been a man of any occupation, if I would not have taken him at a word I would I might go to hell among the rogues. And so he fell. When he came to himself again, he said, if he had done or said anything amiss, he desir'd their worships to think it was his infirmity. Three or four wenches where I stood cried 'Alas, good soul!' and forgave him with all their hearts. But there's no heed to be taken of them. If Caesar had stabb'd their mothers, they would have done no less. 263

BRU.   And after that, he came thus sad away?

---

235. **fain:** gladly. 238. **still as he refused it:** every time he refused it. 239. **hooted:** shouted (in approbation).—**chopt:** chapped, raw. [S.H.] 241. **swoonded:** swooned, fainted. This incident is of Shakespeare's own invention, but he got the hint from Plutarch. 244. **soft:** literally "slow," "slowly." 247. **the falling sickness:** epilepsy, to which Caesar had been subject from his youth. Cassius then repeats the expression, this time alluding to the lower stature of Brutus, Casca and himself. [S.H.] 251. **tag-rag:** low. 253. **true:** honest. 256. **doublet:** a short jacket. [S.H.] 257. **An:** if.— **a man of any occupation:** a tradesman, one of the plebeians there present. 258. **taken him at a word:** taken him at his word instantly. 260. **his infirmity:** the falling sickness. 261. **wenches:** young women.

---

†   Bradley again chooses to visualize the content of this speech. The spectators are offered a view of Caesar being offered the crown thrice by Antony, then falling onto the ground in a high-angle shot that emphasizes his weakness. [S.H.]

| | | |
|---|---|---|
| CASCA | Ay. | 265 |
| CASS. | Did Cicero say anything? | |
| CASCA | Ay, he spoke Greek. | |
| CASS. | To what effect? | |

CASCA    Nay, an I tell you that, I'll ne'er look you i' th' face again. But those that understood him smil'd at one another and shook their heads; but for mine own part, it was Greek to me. I could tell you more news too. Marullus and Flavius, for pulling scarfs off Caesar's images, are put to silence. Fare you well. There was more foolery yet, if I could remember it.    273

CASS.    Will you sup with me tonight, Casca?

CASCA    No, I am promis'd forth.    275

CASS.    Will you dine with me tomorrow?

CASCA    Ay, if I be alive, and your mind hold, and your dinner worth the eating.

CASS.    Good. I will expect you.

CASCA    Do so. Farewell both.

BRU.    What a blunt fellow is this grown to be!    280
He was quick mettle when he went to school.

CASS.    So is he now in execution
Of any bold or noble enterprise,
However he puts on this tardy form.
This rudeness is a sauce to his good wit,    285
Which gives men stomach to digest his words
With better appetite.

BRU.    And so it is. For this time I will leave you.
Tomorrow, if you please to speak with me,
I will come home to you; or if you will,    290
Come home to me, and I will wait for you.

CASS.    I will do so. Till then, think of the world.    *Exit* Brutus.
Well, Brutus, thou art noble; yet I see
Thy honorable mettle may be wrought
From that it is dispos'd. Therefore it is meet    295

---

268. **To what effect?** "What was the purport of his speech?" 269. **I'll n'er look you i' th' face again:** I'll never be able to look at you straight in the eyes again. [S.H.] 271. **Greek to me:** Proverbial for anything unintelligible. 272. **put to silence:** suppressed, forbidden to take any part in public affairs. 280. **blunt:** dull, slowwitted. 281. **He was quick mettle:** He was of an apt and ready quality or temper. 284. **However:** however much, although.—**this tardy form:** this appearance of stupidity. 286. **stomach:** appetite or inclination. [S.H.] 292. **the world:** the way things are. [S.H.] 294. **wrought:** so worked upon as to acquire a quality quite different from its native disposition. 295. **From:** "away from" and so "contrary to." **that:** what.

That noble minds keep ever with their likes;
For who so firm that cannot be seduc'd?
Caesar doth bear me hard; but he loves Brutus.
If I were Brutus now and he were Cassius,
He should not humor me. I will this night,                    300
In several hands, in at his windows throw,
As if they came from several citizens,
Writings, all tending to the great opinion
That Rome holds of his name; wherein obscurely
Caesar's ambition shall be glanced at.                        305
And after this let Caesar seat him sure,
For we will shake him, or worse days endure.†        *Exit.*

### SCENE III. [*Rome. A street.*]

*Thunder and lightning.‡ Enter, [from opposite sides,] Casca, [with his sword drawn,] and Cicero.*

---

298. **doth bear me hard:** looks upon me with disfavor. 300. **humor:** cajole, win over by the arts of flattery. Cassius prides himself upon being unassailable by artful persuasion. 301. **hands:** handwriting. 305. **glanced at:** hinted at, touched upon indirectly. 306. **seat him sure:** secure himself. [S.H.] 307. The scene ends with a rhyming couplet, as is very often the case in the Elizabethan drama. Such a formal close not only gave the actor a good mouth-filling speech for his exit, but also helped to mark the boundaries between acts and scenes. The old theaters had no shifting scenery and no drop-curtain.

**SCENE III.**

Scene 3 takes place on the night of March 14—the night before the Ides of March. For dramatic reasons, Shakespeare suppresses the interval between the Lupercalia (15 February) and the eve of the Ides of March. [S.H.]

---

† In Bradley's 1950 version, Cassius delivers the last speech of the scene while walking between two endless rows of columns. This setting accentuates the magnificence of Rome but also creates a feeling of doom, as if the characters were now enclosed and trapped by fatality in one single way of action. The same effect is created in Mankiewicz's 1953 version, but with different means: Cassius walks quickly and intently toward a camera which keeps back-tracking, as if pushed by a course of action that was now set in motion and impossible to interrupt. This speech of Cassius is immediately followed by strong winds and lightning, as if the words themselves had given birth to the ominous storm. In the 1970 Burge production, Cassius tempestuously takes the flowers away from Caesar's bust, while baleful, frantic music breaks in to announce the storm. Both Mankiewicz and Burge have, therefore, chosen to create a very explicit link between Cassius's conspiratorial mood and the sinister storm to come. [S.H.]

‡ On screen, the storm scene has been turned into spectacular sequences. In Bradley's film, Cassius, Casca and Cinna appear in chiaroscuro close-ups, their faces regularly revealed by the frequent flashes of lightning. In Mankiewicz's version, Cassius, his face covered by a hood, arrives amidst the flashes. Filmed with a low-angle shot, he breaks through darkness like a malevolent witch. In Bradley's and Mankiewicz's visions, the whole sequence is based on a contrast between light and shadow, and revels in a spirit of conspiratorial terror. Burge's production is less expressionistic. It features a very realistic and dramatic storm scene, stressing the exceptional aspect of the weather—dogs almost drowning in puddles, people screaming and running for shelter under a pelting rain. [S.H.]

| | |
|---|---|
| CIC. | Good even, Casca. Brought you Caesar home? |
| | Why are you breathless? And why stare you so? |

| | | |
|---|---|---|
| CASCA | Are not you mov'd when all the sway of earth | |
| | Shakes like a thing unfirm? O Cicero, | |
| | I have seen tempests when the scolding winds | 5 |
| | Have riv'd the knotty oaks, and I have seen | |
| | Th' ambitious ocean swell and rage and foam | |
| | To be exalted with the threat'ning clouds; | |
| | But never till tonight, never till now, | |
| | Did I go through a tempest dropping fire. | 10 |
| | Either there is a civil strife in heaven, | |
| | Or else the world, too saucy with the gods, | |
| | Incenses them to send destruction. | |

| | |
|---|---|
| CIC. | Why, saw you any thing more wonderful? |

| | | |
|---|---|---|
| CASCA | A common slave (you know him well by sight) | 15 |
| | Held up his left hand, which did flame and burn | |
| | Like twenty torches join'd; and yet his hand, | |
| | Not sensible of fire, remain'd unscorch'd. | |
| | Besides (I ha' not since put up my sword), | |
| | Against the Capitol I met a lion, | 20 |
| | Who glar'd upon me, and went surly by | |
| | Without annoying me. And there were drawn | |
| | Upon a heap a hundred ghastly women, | |
| | Transformed with their fear, who swore they saw | |
| | Men, all in fire, walk up and down the streets. | 25 |
| | And yesterday the bird of night did sit | |
| | Even at noonday upon the market place, | |
| | Hooting and shrieking. When these prodigies | |
| | Do so conjointly meet, let not men say | |
| | 'These are their reasons—they are natural,' | 30 |
| | For I believe they are portentous things | |
| | Unto the climate that they point upon. | |

| | | |
|---|---|---|
| CIC. | Indeed it is a strange-disposed time. | |
| | But men may construe things after their fashion, | |
| | Clean from the purpose of the things themselves. | 35 |

---

1. **Brought:** escorted. 3. **all the sway of earth:** the whole sovereign power of earth. 6. **riv'd:** split. [S.H.] 8. **exalted with:** raised as high as. [S.H.] 12. **saucy:** insolent. [S.H.] 14. **more wonderful:** more wonderful than the storm itself. 18. **sensible of:** sensitive to. [S.H.] 19. **put up:** sheathed. 20. **Against:** opposite. 21. **glar'd:** stared glassily.—**surly:** morosely. [S.H.] 22. **annoying:** harming. 22-23. **drawn Upon a heap:** huddled together. 26. **the bird of night:** the owl, a notoriously ill-omened creature. 28. **prodigies:** omens. [S.H.] 29. **conjointly meet:** coincide in time and place and agree in their apparent meaning. 32. **climate:** region. 33. **strange-disposed:** abnormal, extraordinary. 34. **construe things after their fashion:** interpret things in their own way. 35. **Clean from the purpose:** in a way utterly opposed to the real meaning.

Comes Caesar to the Capitol tomorrow?

CASCA    He doth; for he did bid Antonius
Send word to you he would be there tomorrow.

CIC.    Good night then, Casca. This disturbed sky
Is not to walk in.

CASCA                    Farewell, Cicero.                    *Exit* Cicero.    40

*Enter* Cassius.

CASS.    Who's there?

CASCA                A Roman.

CASS.                            Casca, by your voice.

CASCA    Your ear is good. Cassius, what night is this!

CASS.    A very pleasing night to honest men.

CASCA    Who ever knew the heavens menace so?

CASS.    Those that have known the earth so full of faults.    45
For my part, I have walk'd about the streets,
Submitting me unto the perilous night,
And, thus unbraced, Casca, as you see,
Have bar'd my bosom to the thunder-stone;
And when the cross blue lightning seem'd to open    50
The breast of heaven, I did present myself
Even in the aim and very flash of it.

CASCA    But wherefore did you so much tempt the heavens?
It is the part of men to fear and tremble
When the most mighty gods by tokens send    55
Such dreadful heralds to astonish us.

CASS.    You are dull, Casca, and those sparks of life
That should be in a Roman you do want,
Or else you use not. You look pale, and gaze,
And put on fear, and cast yourself in wonder,    60
To see the strange impatience of the heavens;
But if you would consider the true cause—
Why all these fires, why all these gliding ghosts,

---

43. **honest:** honorable. 48. **unbraced:** with my doublet unbuttoned and open. 49. **thunder-stone:** thunderbolt—a fiery bolt, or stone missile, supposed to be discharged from the clouds by the thunder and to destroy whatever it strikes. 50. **cross:** zigzag. 53. **tempt:** try, test. 55. **tokens:** ominous signs. 56. **astonish:** to stun us with a sense of their power, to smite us with fear and awe. 57. **life:** intellectual life, mental alertness. 58. **want:** lack. [S.H.] 60. **cast yourself in wonder:** throw yourself into a state of unreasoning amazement. 61. **impatience:** violence, turmoil.

Why birds and beasts, from quality and kind;
Why old men fool and children calculate;                65
Why all these things change from their ordinance,
Their natures, and preformed faculties,
To monstrous quality—why, you shall find
That heaven hath infus'd them with these spirits
To make them instruments of fear and warning          70
Unto some monstrous state.
Now could I, Casca, name to thee a man
Most like this dreadful night
That thunders, lightens, opens graves, and roars
As doth the lion in the Capitol;                       75
A man no mightier than thyself or me
In personal action, yet prodigious grown
And fearful, as these strange eruptions are.

CASCA    'Tis Caesar that you mean. Is it not, Cassius?

CASS.    Let it be who it is. For Romans now            80
Have thews and limbs like to their ancestors;
But woe the while! our fathers' minds are dead,
And we are govern'd with our mothers' spirits;
Our yoke and sufferance show us womanish.

CASCA    Indeed, they say the senators tomorrow          85
Mean to establish Caesar as a king,
And he shall wear his crown by sea and land
In every place save here in Italy.

CASS.    I know where I will wear this dagger then;
Cassius from bondage will deliver Cassius.             90
Therein, ye gods, you make the weak most strong;
Therein, ye gods, you tyrants do defeat.
Nor stony tower, nor walls of beaten brass,
Nor airless dungeon, nor strong links of iron,

---

64. **from quality and kind:** contrary to their characteristic quality. 65. **Why...calculate:** why old men, who are naturally wise, act and talk like fools, and children, who are naturally foolish, show prophetic wisdom. 66. **their ordinance:** their established order. 67. **preformed faculties:** established functions. 68. **monstrous quality:** a character that is abnormal, strange, contrary to nature.—**you shall find:** you will certainly find. 69. **these spirits:** these [unnatural] dispositions or tendencies. 71. **some monstrous state:** some government or commonwealth that is in an abnormal condition. 75. **the lion in the Capitol:** Shakespeare was doubtless thinking of the lions in the Tower of London. They were one of the sights of the city and gave rise to the idiom "to see the lions" ("to see the sights of London"). 77. **prodigious:** threatening and ominous. 78. **eruptions:** outbursts of the violent forces of nature. 81. **thews:** sinews. 82. **woe the while!** An exclamation of grief and regret, meaning literally, "woe be to the time!" 83. **with:** by.—**spirits:** dispositions. 84. **Our yoke and sufferance:** not merely the fact that we wear the yoke, but that we wear it patiently.—**sufferance:** tame endurance. 87. **he shall wear:** he is to wear. 92. **defeat:** thwart. 93. **stony:** made of stone.

Can be retentive to the strength of spirit;                           95
But life, being weary of these worldly bars,
Never lacks power to dismiss itself.
If I know this, know all the world besides,
That part of tyranny that I do bear
I can shake off at pleasure.                    *Thunder still.*

CASCA                    So can I.                              100
So every bondman in his own hand bears
The power to cancel his captivity.

CASS.    And why should Caesar be a tyrant then?
Poor man! I know he would not be a wolf
But that he sees the Romans are but sheep;                            105
He were no lion, were not Romans hinds.
Those that with haste will make a mighty fire
Begin it with weak straws. What trash is Rome,
What rubbish and what offal, when it serves
For the base matter to illuminate                                     110
So vile a thing as Caesar! But, O grief,
Where hast thou led me? I, perhaps, speak this
Before a willing bondman. Then I know
My answer must be made. But I am arm'd,
And dangers are to me indifferent.                                   115

CASCA    You speak to Casca, and to such a man
That is no fleering telltale. Hold, my hand.
Be factious for redress of all these griefs,
And I will set this foot of mine as far
As who goes farthest.

CASS.                    There's a bargain made.             120
Now know you, Casca, I have mov'd already
Some certain of the noblest-minded Romans
To undergo with me an enterprise
Of honorable-dangerous consequence;

---

95. **Can...spirit:** can confine a strong nature. 97. **dismiss:** liberate. 98. **know all the world besides:** let the rest of the world know. [S.H.] 99. **at pleasure:** when it pleases me to do so, at will. [S.H.] 106. **hinds:** female deer, cowardly creatures. 108-109. **Trash, rubbish,** and **offal** mean practically the same thing—"worthless refuse." Since the kindling of a fire is mentioned, however, Shakespeare doubtless had in mind *trash* in the special sense of "the fragments cut away in trimming a hedge," and *offal* in its literal sense of "that which falls off" (from trees)—waste bits of wood, fit only for kindling. 111. **vile:** worthless. 113. **bondman:** slave. [S.H.] 114. **My answer must be made:** I shall have to answer [to Caesar] for my words. If Casca is a willing bondman, he will act the informer.—**I am arm'd:** i.e., with the power to deliver myself by suicide. 117. **That:** as.—**fleering:** scornful. [S.H.] 118. **factious:** active in forming a party.—**griefs:** grievances. 120. **who:** whoever, any one who. 123. **undergo:** undertake. 124. **consequence:** not "result," but simply "the future."

|  | And I do know, by this they stay for me | 125 |
|---|---|---|
|  | In Pompey's Porch; for now, this fearful night. |  |
|  | There is no stir or walking in the streets, |  |
|  | And the complexion of the element |  |
|  | In favor's like the work we have in hand, |  |
|  | Most bloody, fiery, and most terrible. | 130 |

*Enter* Cinna.

CASCA    Stand close awhile, for here comes one in haste.

CASS.    'Tis Cinna. I do know him by his gait.
He is a friend. Cinna, where haste you so?

CIN.    To find out you. Who's that? Metellus Cimber?

CASS.    No, it is Casca, one incorporate                    135
To our attempts. Am I not stay'd for, Cinna?

CIN.    I am glad on't. What a fearful night is this!
There's two or three of us have seen strange sights.

CASS.    Am I not stay'd for? Tell me.

CIN.                    Yes, you are.
O Cassius, if you could                                        140
But win the noble Brutus to our party—

CASS.    Be you content. Good Cinna, take this paper
And look you lay it in the praetor's chair,
Where Brutus may but find it. And throw this
In at his window. Set this up with wax                        145
Upon old Brutus' statue. All this done,
Repair to Pompey's Porch, where you shall find us.
Is Decius Brutus and Trebonius there?

CIN.    All but Metellus Cimber, and he's gone
To seek you at your house. Well, I will hie                   150
And so bestow these papers as you bade me.

CASS.    That done, repair to Pompey's Theater.    *Exit* Cinna.

---

125. **by this:** by this time.—**stay:** wait [S.H.] 126. **Pompey's Porch:** Pompey's portico or colonnade, attached to Pompey's Theater in the Campus Martius. 128. **the complexion of the element:** the condition of the sky. 129. **In favor's like:** in appearance like. 131. **close:** in concealment. 135. **incorporate:** so united with us as to form a part of the same body. 136. **stay'd for:** waited for. [S.H.] 137. **on't:** of it. 142. **Be you content:** Be easy in mind about that. 143. **chair:** chair in which Brutus would sit when delivering judgment as **praetor**—a magistrate next in rank to a consul. 144. **may but:** must surely. [S.H.] 147. **repair:** make your way. [S.H.] 148. **Decius Brutus:** a mistake for Decimus Brutus. Shakespeare derived the error from North's Plutarch. 150. **hie:** go quickly. [S.H.] 151. **bestow:** deposit, place.

Come, Casca, you and I will yet ere day
See Brutus at his house. Three parts of him
Is ours already, and the man entire                                    155
Upon the next encounter yields him ours.

CASCA    O, he sits high in all the people's hearts;
And that which would appear offense in us,
His countenance, like richest alchemy,
Will change to virtue and to worthiness.                               160

CASS.    Him and his worth and our great need of him
You have right well conceited. Let us go,
For it is after midnight; and ere day
We will awake him and be sure of him.                    *Exeunt.*

# ACT II

### SCENE I. [*Rome.*]

*Enter* Brutus *in his orchard.*

BRU.     What, Lucius, ho!
I cannot by the progress of the stars
Give guess how near to day. Lucius, I say!
I would it were my fault to sleep so soundly.
When, Lucius, when? Awake, I say! What, Lucius!        5

*Enter* Lucius.

LUC.     Call'd you, my lord?

---

156. **encounter:** meeting. 159. **countenance:** approval, support, endorsement. 156. **yields him ours:** wins him as part of our conspiracy. [S.H.] 159. **alchemy:** Casca is saying: "As the art of alchemy, in its richest (or most powerful) operation, changes base metals into gold, so the approval and support of Brutus will change what, *in us,* would be thought crime, into virtuous action and honorable conduct." 160. **worthiness:** honorable conduct. 162. **conceited:** conceived, understood.—**go:** i.e., to the rendezvous at Pompey's Porch. They intend to call on Brutus after the general meeting of the conspirators.

**ACT II. SCENE I.**

In the interval between the acts Cassius has taken Casca to the meeting of the conspirators at Pompey's Theater. Cinna has joined them there after disposing of the papers given him by Cassius. Scene I opens a little before dawn on the ides (the 15th) of March. The place is Brutus's orchard—the garden attached to his house. Brutus has just risen after a sleepless night (2.1.88). 2. **stars:** The storm has ceased and the stars are visible, but the face of the sky is a blaze of meteors (2.1.44). 5. **When, Lucius, when?** *When* and *what* were common interjections of impatience or of urgent summons.

BRU.    Get me a taper in my study, Lucius.
        When it is lighted, come and call me here.

LUC.    I will, my lord.

BRU.    It must be by his death; and for my part, †                    10
        I know no personal cause to spurn at him,
        But for the general. He would be crown'd.
        How that might change his nature, there's the question.
        It is the bright day that brings forth the adder,
        And that craves wary walking. Crown him—that!               15
        And then I grant we put a sting in him
        That at his will he may do danger with.
        Th' abuse of greatness is, when it disjoins
        Remorse from power. And to speak truth of Caesar,
        I have not known when his affections sway'd                 20
        More than his reason. But 'tis a common proof
        That lowliness is young ambition's ladder,
        Whereto the climber-upward turns his face;
        But when he once attains the upmost round,
        He then unto the ladder turns his back,                     25
        Looks in the clouds, scorning the base degrees
        By which he did ascend. So Caesar may.

---

7. **taper:** candle. [S.H.] 11. **spurn:** kick violently. [S.H.] 12. **for the general:** with reference to the people at large. 14. **brings forth:** As a sunny day tempts the adder forth from his lurking place into the public path, so unlimited power may bring out the latent evil in Caesar's character. 15. **craves:** requires. 16. **put a sting in him:** give him power to do harm. [S.H.] 17. **danger:** harm. 18-19. **Th' abuse...power:** The misuse of authority comes ordinarily from the fact that absolute rulers forget what mercy means. *Remorse* is compassion, mercy. 20. **affections:** feelings and impulses in general. Caesar, Brutus thinks, has never been swayed (dominated) by passion. Hence, perhaps, he will not lose his equilibrium when he becomes all-powerful. 21. **a common proof:** a matter of common experience, and therefore to be feared in Caesar's case. 22. **lowliness:** humility (the opposite of *arrogance*). 24. **round:** rung. [S.H.] 26. **base degrees:** the lower steps or rungs of the ladder—with a suggestion also of grades of office. 27. **So Caesar may:** He may lose all his care for the commons, all his devotion to their interests, and become a mere tyrant.

---

†    This monologue has been treated very differently by the film directors. In Bradley's 1950 version, Brutus's face is seen in extreme close-up in the dark while he delivers the monologue in voice-over. The character is filmed while he does not speak but thinks. The spectators learn his secret thoughts as if entering his brain. With this technique based on a major filmic convention, the cinema imitates the way we listen to our own conscience. The voice-over literally becomes the voice of the mind. In Mankiewicz's 1953 film, Brutus is walking slowly in his orchard. The camera films him behind the thin branches of a tree, creating a metaphorical net in which he is entangling himself. The shape of the branches also reminds us of the flashes of lightning, thus creating an aesthetic link with the previous storm scene. As Brutus, James Mason speaks the words aloud. The monologue becomes an emotional as well as physical event that the character goes through, listening to his own voice. In the BBC version (1979), director Herbert Wise prefers to alternate the two techniques—voice-over and loud voice—and provides the example of a subtle transition from verbal to mental over the course of the monologue, which is transformed into a quasi-dialogue between Brutus and himself. [S.H.]

Then lest he may, prevent. And since the quarrel
Will bear no color for the thing he is,
Fashion it thus: that what he is, augmented,                    30
Would run to these and these extremities;
And therefore think him as a serpent's egg,
Which, hatch'd, would as his kind grow mischievous,
And kill him in the shell.

*Enter* Lucius.

LUC.    The taper burneth in your closet, sir.                  35
        Searching the window for a flint, I found
        This paper, thus seal'd up; and I am sure
        It did not lie there when I went to bed.    *Gives him the letter.*

BRU.    Get you to bed again; it is not day.
        Is not tomorrow, boy, the ides of March?               40

LUC.    I know not, sir.

BRU.    Look in the calendar and bring me word.

LUC.    I will, sir.                                           *Exit.*

BRU.    The exhalations, whizzing in the air,
        Give so much light that I may read by them.            45

                                *Opens the letter and reads.*

        'Brutus, thou sleep'st. Awake, and see thyself!
        Shall Rome, &c. Speak, strike, redress!'

        'Brutus, thou sleep'st. Awake!'
        Such instigations have been often dropp'd
        Where I have took them up.                             50
        'Shall Rome, &c.' Thus must I piece it out:
        Shall Rome stand under one man's awe? What, Rome?
        My ancestors did from the streets of Rome

---

28. **prevent:** forestall, take measures to anticipate the danger. *Prevent* in Elizabethan English always retains the literal sense of "anticipating."—**the quarrel:** the cause of complaint, the case against Caesar as a man. 29. **bear no color:** carry no appearance of justice. 30. **Fashion it thus:** state the case as follows. 31. **extremities:** extremes, conclusions, severities. [S.H.] 33. **as his kind:** like the rest of his breed.— **mischievous:** harmful. 35. **closet:** study. 44. **exhalations:** meteors, formerly ascribed to the combustion of gases exhaled from the heavenly bodies. The meteors in question were amongst the omens which were said to have portended the death of Caesar. 45. **them** (emphatic): I do not need the taper, and can read this paper without retiring to my study. 46-47. The letter prepared by Cassius and thrown in at the window by Cinna (1.3.144-145) comes at the decisive moment. Brutus has just convinced himself that Caesar's personal amiability and high-mindedness should be no bar to the murder, but that he must be treated as a dangerous reptile. The letter confirms his decision, for it seems to show that the people share his fears, and, further, it recalls to his mind the whole course of Cassius's argument in 1.2.51-161, and in particular the appeal there made to his pride of ancestry. 47. **redress:** remedy. [S.H.] 51. **Thus must I piece it out:** Brutus fills out the blank in strict accordance with the words of Cassius in 1.2.152-161, which have made a powerful impression on him.

Brutus entangled in his dilemma (Mankiewicz's 1953 film, 2.1.10-34).

The Tarquin drive when he was call'd a king.[†]
'Speak, strike, redress!' Am I entreated                    55
To speak and strike? O Rome, I make thee promise,
If the redress will follow, thou receivest
Thy full petition at the hand of Brutus!

                    *Enter* Lucius.

LUC.   Sir, March is wasted fifteen days.         *Knock within.*

BRU.   'Tis good. Go to the gate; somebody knocks.     [*Exit* Lucius.]   60
        Since Cassius first did whet me against Caesar,
        I have not slept.
        Between the acting of a dreadful thing
        And the first motion, all the interim is

---

56. **I make thee promise:** Brutus doubts and hesitates no longer. He has persuaded himself that the murder is not only a necessity, but an act of the loftiest patriotism, and, besides, that his personal and ancestral honor requires him to be a leader in the conspiracy. 59. **March is wasted fifteen days:** Distinctions between day and night not being marked, as in the modern theater, by darkening the stage, it was necessary for the audience to be informed that the ides or fifteenth of March had come, though day had not dawned. Lucius's phrase is, then, merely a roundabout way of saying, "This is the fifteenth day of the month." 61. **whet:** provoke, goad, incite. [S.H.] 64. **the first motion:** the first proposal of the dreadful thing. *To move* often means to "propose" or "mention."

---

† At this point in Mankiewicz's film, Brutus comes near a bust of Junius Brutus, his famous ancestor who overthrew King Tarquin the Proud in B.C. 509. The film thus creates a visual correlate to help the viewer grasp the meaning of the reference. [S.H.]

Like a phantasma or a hideous dream.                              65
The genius and the mortal instruments
Are then in council, and the state of man,
Like to a little kingdom, suffers then
The nature of an insurrection.

*Enter* Lucius.

LUC.    Sir, 'tis your brother Cassius at the door,              70
        Who doth desire to see you.

BRU.                                        Is he alone?

LUC.    No, sir, there are moe with him.

BRU.                                    Do you know them?

LUC.    No, sir. Their hats are pluck'd about their ears
        And half their faces buried in their cloaks,
        That by no means I may discover them                    75
        By any mark of favor.

BRU.                            Let 'em enter.          [*Exit* Lucius.]
        They are the faction. O conspiracy,
        Sham'st thou to show thy dang'rous brow by night,
        When evils are most free? O, then by day
        Where wilt thou find a cavern dark enough           80
        To mask thy monstrous visage? Seek none, conspiracy.
        Hide it in smiles and affability!
        For if thou path, thy native semblance on,
        Not Erebus itself were dim enough
        To hide thee from prevention.                           85

*Enter the* Conspirators, Cassius, Casca, Decius,
Cinna, Metellus [Cimber], *and* Trebonius.

CASS.   I think we are too bold upon your rest.
        Good morrow, Brutus. Do we trouble you?

---

65. **phantasma:** some wild vision of the disordered imagination. 66–69. **The genius...insurrection:** The *genius*, in Elizabethan usage, commonly means a kind of guardian spirit, inseparable from the man himself and sharing his fortunes. 67. **the state of man:** the man himself conceived as a state or commonwealth, or, as we read in the next line, as a kingdom in miniature. 69. **The nature of an insurrection:** a kind of insurrection. 70. **your brother:** brother-in-law. Cassius had married Junia, Brutus's sister. [S.H.] 72. **moe:** others. This is not the same word as *more* but an independent formation from the same root. 76. **favor:** feature. 77. **the faction:** the party. 83. **path:** walk, take thy way; the whole phrase, then, means "walk in thy natural guise." 84. **Erebus:** the dark place in the underworld through which the shades of the dead pass on their way to Hades. [S.H.] 85. **prevention:** hindrance by anticipation. 86. **too bold upon your rest:** too bold in thus intruding upon your time of sleep. 87. **Good morrow:** good morning. This was the regular salutation until noon, after which "good even" was used.

| | |
|---|---|
| BRU. | I have been up this hour, awake all night. |
| | Know I these men that come along with you? |
| CASS. | Yes, every man of them; and no man here    90 |
| | But honors you; and every one doth wish |
| | You had but that opinion of yourself |
| | Which every noble Roman bears of you. |
| | This is Trebonius. |
| BRU. | He is welcome hither. |
| CASS. | This, Decius Brutus. |
| BRU. | He is welcome too.    95 |
| CASS. | This, Casca; this, Cinna; and this, Metellus Cimber. |
| BRU. | They are all welcome. |
| | What watchful cares do interpose themselves |
| | Betwixt your eyes and night? |
| CASS. | Shall I entreat a word?    *They whisper.*† 100 |
| DEC. | Here lies the east. Doth not the day break here? |
| CASCA | No. |
| CIN. | O, pardon, sir, it doth; and yon grey lines |
| | That fret the clouds are messengers of day. |
| CASCA | You shall confess that you are both deceiv'd.    105 |
| | Here, as I point my sword, the sun arises,‡ |
| | Which is a great way growing on the south, |
| | Weighing the youthful season of the year. |
| | Some two months hence, up higher toward the north |
| | He first presents his fire; and the high east    110 |
| | Stands as the Capitol, directly here. |

---

95. **Decius:** this should be *Decimus*. See note on 1.3.148. 98. **watchful cares:** anxiety causing sleeplessness. [S.H.] 100. Brutus and Cassius step aside, and, in this private conference, Cassius answers the question asked by Brutus and explains the present state of the plot, informing Brutus that all present have joined the "faction." While Brutus and Cassius confer, the others courteously occupy themselves with casual talk. 104. **fret:** interlace. [S.H.] 107. **growing on:** tending toward. 108. **Weighing:** considering. The sense is, "If you consider that it is now early spring, the beginning of the year, you will remember that the sun must be in the south." 111. **as the Capitol:** as the Capitol does.

---

†   This moment when Brutus and Cassius talk in private can be played very differently. In Bradley's version, it is still possible to see them discussing in the background. The same applies for the BBC production. However, in Mankiewicz's film, the spectators cannot witness their interview. We are left with the other conspirators only. [S.H.]

‡   In Mankiewicz's production, Casca utters those lines while pointing his sword toward Brutus. The meaning is made clear: according to Casca, Brutus will arise, as a new sun, to free Rome from tyranny. [S.H.]

| | |
|---|---|
| Bru. | Give me your hands all over, one by one. |
| Cass. | And let us swear our resolution. |
| Bru. | No, not an oath. If not the face of men, |

The sufferance of our souls, the time's abuse—                    115
If these be motives weak, break off betimes,
And every man hence to his idle bed.
So let high-sighted tyranny range on
Till each man drop by lottery. But if these
(As I am sure they do) bear fire enough                           120
To kindle cowards and to steel with valour
The melting spirits of women, then, countrymen,
What need we any spur but our own cause
To prick us to redress? what other bond
Than secret Romans that have spoke the word                       125
And will not palter? and what other oath
Than honesty to honesty engag'd
That this shall be, or we will fall for it?
Swear priests and cowards and men cautelous,
Old feeble carrions and such suffering souls                      130
That welcome wrongs; unto bad causes swear
Such creatures as men doubt; but do not stain
The even virtue of our enterprise,
Nor th' insuppressive mettle of our spirits,
To think that or our cause or our performance                     135
Did need an oath; when every drop of blood
That every Roman bears, and nobly bears,
Is guilty of a several bastardy
If he do break the smallest particle
Of any promise that hath pass'd from him.                         140

| | |
|---|---|
| Cass. | But what of Cicero? Shall we sound him? |
| | I think he will stand very strong with us. |

---

114. **the face of men:** the sad and anxious looks of our fellow-citizens. 115. **sufferance:** suffering.—**the time's abuse:** the abuses of these days; in particular, the continual violation of the Roman constitution on the part of Caesar. 116. **motives:** incentives to action.—**betimes:** immediately, without delay. [S.H.] 118. **high-sighted:** haughty, arrogant. 119. **Till…lottery:** until every man worthy of the name has fallen a victim to the capricious enmity of the tyrant. This is the "abuse of greatness" mentioned by Brutus in his soliloquy, when it "disjoins remorse [compassion] from power" (2.1.18-19). 122. **melting spirits:** feeble, yielding temperaments. 124. **prick:** incite. 125. **Than secret Romans:** than the mere fact that we are Romans engaged in a secret enterprise. 126. **palter:** cheat. 127. **honesty:** personal honor.—**engag'd:** pledged. 129. **cautelous:** overcautious, suspicious. 130. **carrions:** physical wrecks.—**suffering:** tame, poor-spirited. 133. **The even virtue:** the uniform and consistent excellence, the unblemished honor. 134. **insuppressive:** indomitable.—**mettle:** see 1.1.58. 135. **To think:** by thinking.—**or…or:** either…or. 138. **a several bastardy:** acts calling into question one's legitimacy as a true, noble Roman. [S.H.] 141. **sound him:** try and discover his opinion. [S.H.]

| CASCA | Let us not leave him out. |
|---|---|
| CIN. | No, by no means. |

| MET. | O, let us have him! for his silver hairs |
| | Will purchase us a good opinion | 145 |
| | And buy men's voices to commend our deeds. |
| | It shall be said his judgment rul'd our hands. |
| | Our youths and wildness shall no whit appear, |
| | But all be buried in his gravity. |

BRU. O, name him not! Let us not break with him;      150
     For he will never follow anything
     That other men begin.

CASS.                 Then leave him out.

CASCA Indeed he is not fit.

DEC. Shall no man else be touch'd but only Caesar?

CASS. Decius, well urg'd. I think it is not meet      155
     Mark Antony, so well belov'd of Caesar,
     Should outlive Caesar. We shall find of him
     A shrewd contriver; and you know, his means,
     If he improve them, may well stretch so far
     As to annoy us all; which to prevent,      160
     Let Antony and Caesar fall together.

BRU. Our course will seem too bloody, Caius Cassius,
     To cut the head off and then hack the limbs,
     Like wrath in death and envy afterwards;
     For Antony is but a limb of Caesar.      165
     Let us be sacrificers, but not butchers, Caius.
     We all stand up against the spirit of Caesar,
     And in the spirit of men there is no blood.
     O that we then could come by Caesar's spirit
     And not dismember Caesar! But, alas,      170
     Caesar must bleed for it! And, gentle friends,
     Let's kill him boldly, but not wrathfully;

---

145. **purchase:** procure, win.—**opinion:** reputation. 149. **gravity:** stability and sobriety of character. The word implies also the "weight" or "authority" which belongs to such a character. 150. **O, name him not!** Brutus instantly takes command of the conspirators.—**break with him:** broach the matter to him. 151. **he will never follow:** Cicero's vanity is well known to have been one of the weakest points in his character. 155. **urg'd:** suggested, mentioned. 156. **of:** by. 157. **of him:** in him. 158. **shrewd:** troublesome, dangerous.—**contriver:** schemer. [S.H.] 159. **improve:** utilize. 160. **annoy:** injure.—**prevent:** see 2.1.28, and note. 164. **envy:** malice, malignity. 167–170. Brutus puns solemnly on the word *spirit,* using it now in the sense of "the sentiments and principles" of Caesar, now in the sense of "soul."—**come by:** get at. 171. **gentle:** honorable, noble.

Let's carve him as a dish fit for the gods,
Not hew him as a carcass fit for hounds.
And let our hearts, as subtle masters do,                    175
Stir up their servants to an act of rage
And after seem to chide 'em. This shall make
Our purpose necessary, and not envious;
Which so appearing to the common eyes,
We shall be call'd purgers, not murderers.                   180
And for Mark Antony, think not of him;
For he can do no more than Caesar's arm
When Caesar's head is off.

CASS.                           Yet I fear him;
For in the ingrafted love he bears to Caesar—

BRU.      Alas, good Cassius, do not think of him!            185
If he love Caesar, all that he can do
Is to himself—take thought, and die for Caesar.
And that were much he should; for he is given
To sports, to wildness, and much company.

TREB.     There is no fear in him. Let him not die;          190
For he will live, and laugh at this hereafter.   *Clock strikes.*

BRU.      Peace! Count the clock.

CASS.                           The clock hath stricken three.

TREB.     'Tis time to part.

CASS.                           But it is doubtful yet
Whether Caesar will come forth today or no;
For he is superstitious grown of late,                       195
Quite from the main opinion he held once
Of fantasy, of dreams, and ceremonies.
It may be these apparent prodigies,
The unaccustom'd terror of this night,
And the persuasion of his augurers                           200

---

176. **servants:** In this simile, the *hearts* correspond to the masters and the *hands* to the servants. They are not to be angry in their hearts, though their hands perform a necessary "act of rage." 177-178. **This...  envious:** This course of action will surely make the deed appear (as it really is) an act of necessity, not the result of malice or private enmity. *Envious* often means "malicious," "malignant." 180. **purgers:** those who purify and heal through bleeding a patient. [S.H.] 183. **Yet:** yet after all, yet in spite of all you say. 184. **ingrafted:** so deeply implanted as to be a part of himself. 187. **take thought and die:** fall into melancholy and pine away. 190. **no fear:** no cause for fear (on our part). 196. **from the main opinion he held once:** contrary to the strong opinion which he once held. Caesar, who professed the Epicurean philosophy, was convinced of the futility of signs and omens. 197. **fantasy:** fancy (which is merely *fant'sy*); hence, in this passage, signs and omens that affect the imagination, imaginary terrors.—**ceremonies:** omens, portents, supernatural indications. 198. **apparent:** manifest, striking. 200. **augurers:** those who practiced divination according to omens. [S.H.]

|       | May hold him from the Capitol today. |       |
|-------|--------------------------------------|-------|
| DEC.  | Never fear that. If he be so resolv'd, | |

DEC.　Never fear that. If he be so resolv'd,
　　　I can o'ersway him; for he loves to hear
　　　That unicorns may be betray'd with trees
　　　And bears with glasses, elephants with holes,　　　205
　　　Lions with toils, and men with flatterers;
　　　But when I tell him he hates flatterers,
　　　He says he does, being then most flattered.
　　　Let me work;
　　　For I can give his humor the true bent　　　　210
　　　And I will bring him to the Capitol.

CASS.　Nay, we will all of us be there to fetch him.

BRU.　By the eighth hour. Is that the uttermost?

CIN.　Be that the uttermost, and fail not then.

MET.　Caius Ligarius doth bear Caesar hard,　　　　215
　　　Who rated him for speaking well of Pompey.
　　　I wonder none of you have thought of him.

BRU.　Now, good Metellus, go along by him.
　　　He loves me well, and I have given him reasons.
　　　Send him but hither, and I'll fashion him.　　　220

CASS.　The morning comes upon's. We'll leave you, Brutus.
　　　And, friends, disperse yourselves; but all remember
　　　What you have said and show yourselves true Romans.

BRU.　Good gentlemen, look fresh and merrily.
　　　Let not our looks put on our purposes,　　　　225
　　　But bear it as our Roman actors do,
　　　With untir'd spirits and formal constancy.
　　　And so good morrow to you every one.　　*Exeunt. Manet Brutus.*
　　　Boy! Lucius! Fast asleep? It is no matter.
　　　Enjoy the honey-heavy dew of slumber.　　　　230

---

203. **o'ersway:** overcome by persuasion. 204. **trees:** The story was that the hunter dodges behind a tree when the unicorn charges, so that the creature's horn sticks fast in the trunk. 205. **glasses:** i.e., mirrors, which attract the bear's gaze and enable the hunter to approach him unperceived.—**holes:** pitfalls—deep pits covered with a layer of boughs and turf.—**toils:** nets or snares. 210. **humor:** feelings, disposition.—**bent:** direction, inclination. 212. **fetch:** escort. It was customary for the friends of distinguished Romans to call upon them in the morning, to enquire after their health or to escort them to the Senate House or elsewhere. 213. **uttermost:** latest. [S.H.] 215. **doth bear Caesar hard:** has a grudge against Caesar. 216. **rated:** berated. 218. **by him:** by his house. 220. **fashion:** mold (to our will). 221. **upon's:** upon us. 224. **fresh:** bright—the opposite to "careworn," "anxious." 225. **put on our purposes:** wear or show our designs. 226-227. **bear it...constancy:** conduct the affair, as our actors play their parts, with unflagging energy and unruffled self-possession. 228. **Manet:** remains. 230. **the honey-heavy dew:** Sleep is often called "dew," because it is conceived as falling gently and imperceptibly from above.

Thou hast no figures nor no fantasies
Which busy care draws in the brains of men;
Therefore thou sleep'st so sound.

*Enter* Portia.

POR.                                        Brutus, my lord!

BRU.    Portia! What mean you? Wherefore rise you now?
It is not for your health thus to commit                    235
Your weak condition to the raw cold morning.

POR.    Nor for yours neither. Y' have ungently, Brutus,
Stole from my bed. And yesternight at supper
You suddenly arose and walk'd about,
Musing and sighing with your arms across;                  240
And when I ask'd you what the matter was,
You star'd upon me with ungentle looks.
I urg'd you further; then you scratch'd your head
And too impatiently stamp'd with your foot.
Yet I insisted; yet you answer'd not,                      245
But with an angry wafture of your hand
Gave sign for me to leave you. So I did,
Fearing to strengthen that impatience
Which seem'd too much enkindled, and withal
Hoping it was but an effect of humor,                      250
Which sometime hath his hour with every man.
It will not let you eat nor talk nor sleep,
And could it work so much upon your shape
As it hath much prevail'd on your condition,
I should not know you Brutus. Dear my lord,                255
Make me acquainted with your cause of grief.

BRU.    I am not well in health, and that is all.

POR.    Brutus is wise and, were he not in health,
He would embrace the means to come by it.

BRU.    Why, so I do. Good Portia, go to bed.              260

---

231. **no figures nor no fantasies:** no [anxious] ideas or fancies. 235. **commit:** expose. 236. **condition:** constitution, state of health. 237. **ungently:** discourteously. 238. **stole:** sneaked away. [S.H.] 240. **across:** folded. 246. **wafture:** waving. [S.H.] 249. **withal:** at the same time, besides. 250. **an effect of humor:** a symptom of some passing mood. 251. **his:** its. 254. **condition:** disposition. 255. **know you Brutus:** recognize you as Brutus. [S.H.] 256. **your cause of grief:** the cause of your grief. 259. **to come by it:** to obtain it (your health).

| | |
|---|---|
| POR. | Is Brutus sick, and is it physical |
| | To walk unbraced and suck up the humors |
| | Of the dank morning? What, is Brutus sick, |
| | And will he steal out of his wholesome bed |
| | To dare the vile contagion of the night, |
| | And tempt the rheumy and unpurged air, |
| | To add unto his sickness? No, my Brutus. |
| | You have some sick offense within your mind, |
| | Which by the right and virtue of my place |
| | I ought to know of; and upon my knees |
| | I charm you, by my once commended beauty, |
| | By all your vows of love, and that great vow |
| | Which did incorporate and make us one, |
| | That you unfold to me, yourself, your half, |
| | Why you are heavy—and what men tonight |
| | Have had resort to you; for here have been |
| | Some six or seven, who did hide their faces |
| | Even from darkness. |
| BRU. | Kneel not, gentle Portia. |
| POR. | I should not need if you were gentle Brutus. |
| | Within the bond of marriage, tell me, Brutus, |
| | Is it excepted I should know no secrets |
| | That appertain to you? Am I yourself |
| | But, as it were, in sort or limitation? |
| | To keep with you at meals, comfort your bed, |
| | And talk to you sometimes? Dwell I but in the suburbs |
| | Of your good pleasure? If it be no more, |
| | Portia is Brutus' harlot, not his wife. |
| BRU. | You are my true and honorable wife, |
| | As dear to me as are the ruddy drops |
| | That visit my sad heart. |
| POR. | If this were true, then should I know this secret. |
| | I grant I am a woman; but withal |

265

270

275

280

285

290

---

261. **physical:** in accordance with medical principles; good for the health. 262. **unbraced:** with the doublet unbuttoned or unlaced. The word implies carelessness in attire.—**the humors:** the mists and dampness. 265. **contagion:** Night air was supposed to be actually poisonous. 266. **tempt:** risk.—**rheumy:** full of moisture, dank.—**unpurged:** not yet purified from its contagious quality by the rays of the sun. The idea that night air is unwholesome was universal. 268. **sick offense:** sickness that troubles you. 271. **I charm you:** I conjure you, I charge you solemnly. 273. **incorporate:** make us one body. 274. **unfold:** disclose. 275. **heavy:** sad, in low spirits.—**tonight:** this night just past. 276. **had resort to you:** visited you. [S.H.] 283. **in sort or limitation:** after a fashion or in a restricted sense. 284. **keep:** stay, remain. 285. **in the suburbs:** outskirts (in Shakespeare's London, brothels were located outside the town center). [S.H.] 289. **ruddy drops:** blood. [S.H.] 292. **withal:** at the same time.

A woman that Lord Brutus took to wife.
I grant I am a woman; but withal
A woman well-reputed, Cato's daughter.                              295
Think you I am no stronger than my sex,
Being so father'd and so husbanded?
Tell me your counsels; I will not disclose 'em.
I have made strong proof of my constancy,
Giving myself a voluntary wound                                    300
Here, in the thigh.† Can I bear that with patience,
And not my husband's secrets?

BRU.                          O ye gods,
Render me worthy of this noble wife!                    *Knock.*
Hark, hark! One knocks. Portia, go in awhile,
And by-and-by thy bosom shall partake                              305
The secrets of my heart.
All my engagements I will construe to thee,
All the charactery of my sad brows.
Leave me with haste.                            *Exit* Portia.
        Lucius, who's that knocks?

            *Enter* Lucius *and* [Caius] Ligarius.

LUC.    Here is a sick man that would speak with you.              310

BRU.    Caius Ligarius, that Metellus spake of.
        Boy, stand aside. Caius Ligarius, how?

CAIUS.  Vouchsafe good-morrow from a feeble tongue.

BRU.    O, what a time have you chose out, brave Caius,
        To wear a kerchief! Would you were not sick!              315

CAIUS.  I am not sick if Brutus have in hand
        Any exploit worthy the name of honor.

---

295. **Cato's daughter:** Marcus Porcius Cato (B.C. 95-46) was famous for his inflexible morality. He fought with Pompey against Caesar and finally committed suicide rather than be captured. [S.H.] 298. **counsels:** secrets. 299. **constancy:** fortitude. 301. **patience:** calmness, self-control. 307. **my engagements:** the affairs to which I am committed or pledged.—**construe:** interpret, explain fully. 308. **the charactery:** literally, handwriting: "I will explain to you fully the expression of my sad face." 310. **a sick man:** Lucius knows by the kerchief (315) that Ligarius is sick. 312. **how?** how do you do? 313. **Vouchsafe:** deign to accept. 314. **brave:** noble. 315. **To wear a kerchief:** to be out of health. The kerchief was a linen head-cloth regularly worn indoors by women. If a man fell sick, his first act was to wrap his head up in a kerchief for warmth and protection against drafts.

---

†    The Mankiewicz movie removes all mention of the "voluntary wound." So does Burge's version. Bradley's film does include the mention but does not show anything. The BBC 1979 production is the only version that not only includes the whole discussion but also offers an actual sight of the blood trickling down Portia's thigh, thus creating a powerful link between Portia's bleeding and Caesar's future bloody wounds. [S.H.]

BRU.    Such an exploit have I in hand, Ligarius,
        Had you a healthful ear to hear of it.

CAIUS.  By all the gods that Romans bow before,                          320
        I here discard my sickness! [*Throws off his kerchief.*] Soul of Rome!
        Brave son, deriv'd from honorable loins!
        Thou like an exorcist hast conjur'd up
        My mortified spirit. Now bid me run,
        And I will strive with things impossible;                       325
        Yea, get the better of them. What's to do?

BRU.    A piece of work that will make sick men whole.

CAIUS.  But are not some whole that we must make sick?

BRU.    That must we also. What it is, my Caius,
        I shall unfold to thee as we are going                          330
        To whom it must be done.

CAIUS.                          Set on your foot,
        And with a heart new-fir'd I follow you,
        To do I know not what; but it sufficeth
        That Brutus leads me on.                        *Thunder.*

BRU.                    Follow me then.                *Exeunt.*[†]


SCENE II. [*Rome. Caesar's house.*]

*Thunder and lightning. Enter* Julius Caesar, *in his nightgown.*

CAES.   Nor heaven nor earth have been at peace tonight.
        Thrice hath Calphurnia in her sleep cried out

---

322. **Brave:** noble.—**honorable loins:** The reference is to his supposed descent from Lucius Junius Brutus, the Liberator. 323. **exorcist:** a conjurer, one who calls up spirits. 324. **mortified:** deadened, paralyzed.— **spirit:** vitality; strength and energy. Ligarius puns solemnly upon the other meaning of the word (a spiritual being), much as Brutus had done in 2.1.167-170. 326. **What's to do?** What's to be done? 330. **unfold:** disclose. 331. **To whom:** to the house of him to whom.—**Set on:** advance.

SCENE II.

The time of this scene extends from early in the morning of the ides to eight o'clock A.M. (2.2.114). 1. **nightgown:** dressing gown.—**tonight:** last night.

---

†   In Mankiewicz's film, the scene ends with a shot of Portia standing near the bust of Junius Brutus and watching her husband exit with Caius Ligarius. This acts as a reminder of Brutus's revolutionary intent but also establishes a link between this scene and the next, in which another woman, Calphurnia, tries to influence her own husband. [S.H.]

'Help, ho! They murther Caesar!' Who's within?[†]

*Enter a* Servant.

SERV.   My lord?

CAES.   Go bid the priests do present sacrifice,                    5
And bring me their opinions of success.

SERV.   I will, my lord.                                    *Exit.*

*Enter* Calphurnia.

CAL.    What mean you, Caesar? Think you to walk forth?
You shall not stir out of your house today.

CAES.   Caesar shall forth. The things that threaten'd me          10
Ne'er look'd but on my back. When they shall see
The face of Caesar, they are vanished.[‡]

CAL.    Caesar, I never stood on ceremonies,
Yet now they fright me. There is one within,
Besides the things that we have heard and seen,              15
Recounts most horrid sights seen by the watch.
A lioness hath whelped in the streets,

---

5. **present:** immediate. 6. **success:** the outcome, the issue, i.e., of Caesar's political plans. 10. **Caesar shall forth:** throughout the scene Caesar's language and bearing are marked by such pomposity that critics have accused Shakespeare of either misapprehending or misrepresenting him. See, however, Introduction (p. viii). The effect of ostentatious speech is in large part produced by Caesar's use of his own name instead of the first personal pronoun. 13. **stood on ceremonies:** gave heed to omens. 17. **whelped:** given birth. [S.H.]

---

†    These three lines have given rise to many interpolations by the screen directors. In the Mankiewicz production, Calphurnia is observed by Caesar as she experiences her nightmare and screams in her sleep. Caesar's "Who's within?" is the only line kept. It is turned into a panicked exclamation as he runs through the house, afraid that people might attack him instantly. Contrary to Mankiewicz, Bradley and Sturge have both chosen to turn Calphurnia's dream into images. Bradley's version constructs a dream that, in its montage of images, is heavily influenced by the style of Sergei Eisenstein, a Russian film director, who edited scenes with the aim of eliciting emotions through analogies and metaphors. In the film *The Battleship Potemkin* (1926), Eisenstein inserts shots of sculpted lions—the first one is asleep, the second is standing, the third is showing its teeth—to generate the idea of popular rebellion. Bradley takes up on this idea, including four different shots of sculpted lions, a shot of Caesar's statue starting to bleed and a shot of the wet ground where the trickling of rain soon turns into streaks of blood. The dream thus mixes the idea of civil strife, revolution and murder in a series of striking images. In Burge's film, the vision is made much more literal but is made complex through its merging of past, present and future. The dream sequence combines shots of Caesar's bleeding statue, shots of Calphurnia's moving and screaming in her sleep (in superimposition) and images showing events from the past (the Soothsayer's warning at the start of the play) and from the future (Artemidorus's warning, the assassination, the popular rebellion, the civil war). The dream is thus, at the same time, a powerful flashback and flashforward, losing the spectators into a maze of images and sounds from different times and spaces. [S.H.]

‡    As he speaks this, the Caesar in Mankiewicz's film is looking at his own statue. Caesar's bust is overlooking the whole scene, as if Caesar the human being was being ordered to act by his divine image, an alienated self who now controlled his actions. [S.H.]

And graves have yawn'd and yielded up their dead.
Fierce fiery warriors fought upon the clouds
In ranks and squadrons and right form of war,                    20
Which drizzled blood upon the Capitol.
The noise of battle hurtled in the air,
Horses did neigh, and dying men did groan,
And ghosts did shriek and squeal about the streets.
O Caesar, these things are beyond all use,                       25
And I do fear them!

CAES.                                What can be avoided
Whose end is purpos'd by the mighty gods?
Yet Caesar shall go forth; for these predictions
Are to the world in general as to Caesar.

CAL.      When beggars die there are no comets seen;            30
The heavens themselves blaze forth the death of princes.

CAES.     Cowards die many times before their deaths;
The valiant never taste of death but once.
Of all the wonders that I yet have heard,
It seems to me most strange that men should fear,               35
Seeing that death, a necessary end,
Will come when it will come.

                        *Enter a* Servant.

                                What say the augurers?

SERV.     They would not have you to stir forth today.
Plucking the entrails of an offering forth,
They could not find a heart within the beast.                    40

CAES.     The gods do this in shame of cowardice.
Caesar should be a beast without a heart
If he should stay at home today for fear.
No, Caesar shall not. Danger knows full well
That Caesar is more dangerous than he.                           45
We are two lions litter'd in one day,

---

18. **yawn'd:** opened, gaped. [S.H.] 20. **squadrons:** square formations [S.H.]—**right form:** regular order.
22. **hurtled:** *To hurtle* is "to clash," "to dash together." There was a noise of the clash of the battle. 24. **shriek and squeal:** The thin voices of spirits and the blood-curdling shrillness of their tones are often mentioned.
25. **use:** that which is usual; ordinary experience. 26-27. **What...gods?** What event whose fulfillment the gods have purposed can be avoided by mortals? 28. **Yet:** despite all this. 29. **Are to...Caesar:** are addressed, or apply, to the whole world as well as to Caesar. Hence he has no occasion for special concern. 31. **blaze:** both flame and proclaim. [S.H.] 39. **plucking the entrails:** augurers examined the entrails of sacrificed beasts to read the future. [S.H.] 41. **in shame of cowardice:** to make cowards ashamed of themselves. [S.H.] 42. **should be:** would certainly be.

And I the elder and more terrible,
And Caesar shall go forth.

CAL.                          Alas, my lord!
Your wisdom is consum'd in confidence.
Do not go forth today. Call it my fear          50
That keeps you in the house and not your own.
We'll send Mark Antony to the Senate House,
And he shall say you are not well today.
Let me upon my knee prevail in this.

CAES.   Mark Antony shall say I am not well,          55
And for thy humor I will stay at home.

                    *Enter* Decius.

Here's Decius Brutus; he shall tell them so.

DEC.    Caesar, all hail! Good morrow, worthy Caesar!
I come to fetch you to the Senate House.

CAES.   And you are come in very happy time          60
To bear my greeting to the senators
And tell them that I will not come today.
Cannot, is false; and that I dare not, falser:
I will not come today. Tell them so, Decius.

CAL.    Say he is sick.

CAES.             Shall Caesar send a lie?          65
Have I in conquest stretch'd mine arm so far
To be afeard to tell greybeards the truth?
Decius, go tell them Caesar will not come.

DEC.    Most mighty Caesar, let me know some cause,
Lest I be laugh'd at when I tell them so.          70

CAES.   The cause is in my will: I will not come.
That is enough to satisfy the Senate;
But for your private satisfaction,
Because I love you, I will let you know.
Calphurnia here, my wife, stays me at home.          75
She dreamt tonight she saw my statue,
Which, like a fountain with an hundred spouts,
Did run pure blood; and many lusty Romans
Came smiling and did bathe their hands in it.

---

56. **humor:** whim, caprice. 57. **Decius:** Decimus Brutus Albinus (see 1.3.148). 58. **worthy:** noble. 59. **fetch:** cf. 2.1.212. 60. **in very happy time:** at a very opportune moment. 72. **enough to satisfy the Senate:** all the information that the Senate can expect of me. 73. **satisfaction:** full information. 75. **stays:** detains. 76. **tonight:** last night.

And these does she apply for warnings and portents 80
And evils imminent, and on her knee
Hath begg'd that I will stay at home today.

DEC.    This dream is all amiss interpreted;
It was a vision fair and fortunate.
Your statute spouting blood in many pipes, 85
In which so many smiling Romans bath'd,
Signifies that from you great Rome shall suck
Reviving blood, and that great men shall press
For tinctures, stains, relics, and cognizance.
This by Calphurnia's dream is signified. 90

CAES.    And this way have you well expounded it.

DEC.    I have, when you have heard what I can say;
And know it now. The Senate have concluded
To give this day a crown to mighty Caesar.
If you shall send them word you will not come, 95
Their minds may change. Besides, it were a mock
Apt to be render'd, for some one to say
'Break up the Senate till another time,
When Caesar's wife shall meet with better dreams.'†
If Caesar hide himself, shall they not whisper 100
'Lo, Caesar is afraid'?
Pardon me, Caesar; for my dear dear love
To your proceeding bids me tell you this,
And reason to my love is liable.

---

85. **in many pipes:** in large casks. [S.H.] 88-89. **great men...cognizance:** a good instance of "dramatic irony"; for Decius's interpretation, though accepted by Caesar, sounds ominous enough. His language, however, is figurative—and so Caesar understands it: "Great men shall be eager for a share in the fresh lifeblood of prosperity which your rule will infuse into the veins of Rome; and they shall throng about you for that share as eagerly as devotees press forward to dip their handkerchiefs in the blood of a martyr." *Tinctures* and *stains* are synonymous. *Relics* suggests the relics of saints preserved in churches. *Cognizance* indicates an heraldic badge, worn to show that one belongs to the household of some great noble.—**press:** crowd. [S.H.] 97. **Apt:** ready, at hand.—**render'd:** spoken in reply—as a retort. 100. **shall they not whisper?** Will they not be sure to whisper? 103. **proceeding:** advancement. 104. **reason to my love is liable:** My devotion to your interests is such that I must speak frankly, even at the risk of using improper freedom.

---

†    Calphurnia gives another of her shocked reactions in Mankiewicz's film when she hears Decius's remark. She also reveals a very worried look as she brings Caesar his robe. The end of the scene significantly focuses on her as she retreats into her bedroom, closing the huge doors behind her in a sign of sad defeat and resignation. Again, Mankiewicz ends a scene by stressing the woman's point of view on the events. The same applies to Bradley's treatment of the end of this scene: Calphurnia remains alone at the breakfast table, stunned and speechless, and finally lowers her head in despair. [S.H.]

CAES.   How foolish do your fears seem now, Calphurnia!          105
        I am ashamed I did yield to them.
        Give me my robe, for I will go.

        *Enter* Brutus, Ligarius, Metellus, Casca, Trebonius, Cinna, *and* Publius.

        And look where Publius is come to fetch me.

PUB.    Good morrow, Caesar.

CAES.                       Welcome, Publius.
        What, Brutus, are you stirr'd so early too?               110
        Good morrow, Casca. Caius Ligarius,
        Caesar was ne'er so much your enemy
        As that same ague which hath made you lean.
        What is't o'clock?

BRU.                    Caesar, 'tis strucken eight.

CAES.   I thank you for your pains and courtesy.                   115

                       *Enter* Antony.

        See! Antony, that revels long a-nights,
        Is notwithstanding up. Good morrow, Antony.

ANT.    So to most noble Caesar.

CAES.                       Bid them prepare within.
        I am to blame to be thus waited for.
        Now, Cinna. Now, Metellus. What, Trebonius;              120
        I have an hour's talk in store for you;
        Remember that you call on me today;
        Be near me, that I may remember you.

TREB.   Caesar, I will. [*Aside*] And so near will I be
        That your best friends shall wish I had been further.     125

CAES.   Good friends, go in and taste some wine with me,
        And we (like friends) will straightway go together.

BRU.    [*aside*] That every like is not the same, O Caesar,
        The heart of Brutus erns to think upon.          *Exeunt.*

---

107. **robe:** toga. Up to this point Caesar has worn his dressing gown. 108. **fetch:** escort. 112. **your enemy:** Ligarius, who had taken part in the Civil War on Pompey's side, had recently been pardoned by Caesar and restored to civil rights. 113. **ague:** fever. [S.H.] 114. **strucken:** a common form of the past participle. Other forms are *strook, strooken, stroken, stricken.* 119. **to blame:** blame-worthy, in fault. 128. **That every like is not the same:** that every seeming friend is not a true friend. 129. **erns:** grieves, sorrows. The personal friendship of Brutus for Caesar is emphasized.

SCENE III. [*Rome. A street near the Capitol.*]

*Enter* Artemidorus, *[reading a paper].*

ART.     'Caesar, beware of Brutus; take heed of Cassius; come not near Casca;
         have an eye to Cinna; trust not Trebonius; mark well Metellus Cimber;
         Decius Brutus loves thee not; thou hast wrong'd Caius Ligarius. There
         is but one mind in all these men, and it is bent against Caesar. If thou
         beest not immortal, look about you. Security gives way to conspiracy.
         The mighty gods defend thee!                                         6
         'Thy lover,
         'ARTEMIDORUS.'
         Here will I stand till Caesar pass along
         And as a suitor will I give him this.                               10
         My heart laments that virtue cannot live
         Out of the teeth of emulation.
         If thou read this, O Caesar, thou mayst live;
         If not, the Fates with traitors do contrive.†            *Exit.*

SCENE IV. [*Before the house of* Brutus.]

*Enter* Portia *and* Lucius.

POR.     I prithee, boy, run to the Senate House.
         Stay not to answer me, but get thee gone!
         Why dost thou stay?

LUC.                             To know my errand, madam.

POR.     I would have had thee there and here again
         Ere I can tell thee what thou shouldst do there.                    5

---

SCENE III.

"One *Artemidorus*…a Doctor of Rethoricke in the Greeke tongue, who by meanes of his profession was
very familiar with certaine of *Brutus* confederates, and therefore knew the most part of all their practises
against *Caesar*: came and brought him a litle bill written with his owne hand, of all that he ment to tell
him." (North's Plutarch). 4. **bent:** directed. 5. **Security gives way to conspiracy:** carelessness, or freedom
from anxiety [*security* in the literal Latin sense], opens a path to the attacks of conspiracy. 7. **lover:** devoted
friend. 10. **suitor:** petitioner. [S.H.] 12. **emulation:** envy, envious rivalry. 14. **contrive:** conspire. [S.H.]

---

†     In Bradley's film, a shot brings together Artemidorus (seen in the foreground) and the Soothsayer (in
      the background). This deep-focused shot thus merges the two kinds of warning: the prophecy and
      the letter. [S.H.]

[*Aside*] O constancy, be strong upon my side,
Set a huge mountain 'tween my heart and tongue!
I have a man's mind, but a woman's might.
How hard it is for women to keep counsel!
Art thou here yet?

LUC.                    Madam, what should I do?                    10
Run to the Capitol and nothing else? .
And so return to you and nothing else?

POR.    Yes, bring me word, boy, if thy lord look well,
For he went sickly forth; and take good note
What Caesar doth, what suitors press to him.          15
Hark, boy! What noise is that?

LUC.    I hear none, madam.

POR.                    Prithee listen well.
I heard a bustling rumor like a fray,
And the wind brings it from the Capitol.

LUC.    Sooth, madam, I hear nothing.                         20

*Enter the* Soothsayer.

POR.    Come hither, fellow. Which way hast thou been?

SOOTH.    At mine own house, good lady.

POR.    What is't o'clock?

SOOTH.                    About the ninth hour, lady.

POR.    Is Caesar yet gone to the Capitol?

SOOTH.    Madam, not yet. I go to take my stand,          25
To see him pass on to the Capitol.

POR.    Thou hast some suit to Caesar, hast thou not?

SOOTH.    That I have, lady, if it will please Caesar
To be so good to Caesar as to hear me:
I shall beseech him to befriend himself.                   30

POR.    Why, know'st thou any harm's intended towards him?

SOOTH.    None that I know will be, much that I fear may chance.
Good morrow to you. Here the street is narrow.

---

SCENE IV.

6. **constancy:** firmness, self-possession.  8. **might:** physical strength.  9. **to keep counsel:** to keep a secret. Cf. 2.1.298.  18. **bustling rumor:** confused noise, hubbub.—**fray:** fight. [S.H.]  20. **Sooth:** truly.  20. **Soothsayer:** the same prophet who had warned Caesar to beware the ides of March (1.2.18).  23. **the ninth hour:** cf. 2.2.114.  25. **take my stand:** take my place. [S.H.]  31. **any harm's intended:** any harm that is intended.

                    The throng that follows Caesar at the heels,
                    Of senators, of praetors, common suitors,                    35
                    Will crowd a feeble man almost to death.
                    I'll get me to a place more void and there
                    Speak to great Caesar as he comes along.          *Exit.*

POR.            I must go in. Ay me, how weak a thing
                    The heart of woman is! O Brutus,                                40
                    The heavens speed thee in thine enterprise!
                    Sure the boy heard me.—Brutus hath a suit
                    That Caesar will not grant.—O, I grow faint.—
                    Run, Lucius, and commend me to my lord;
                    Say I am merry. Come to me again                            45
                    And bring me word what he doth say to thee.   *Exeunt [severally].*


# ACT III

### SCENE I. [*Rome. A street before the Capitol.*]

*Flourish. Enter* Caesar, Brutus, Cassius, Casca, Decius, Metellus, Trebonius, Cinna,
Antony, Lepidus, Artemidorus, Popilius, Publius, *and the* Soothsayer.

CAES.         The ides of March are come.

SOOTH.      Ay, Caesar, but not gone.

ART.            Hail, Caesar! Read this schedule.

DEC.           Trebonius doth desire you to o'erread
                    (At your best leisure) this his humble suit.                     5

ART.            O Caesar, read mine first; for mine's a suit
                    That touches Caesar nearer. Read it, great Caesar!

CAES.         What touches us ourself shall be last serv'd.

---

35. **praetors:** magistrates next in rank to a consul; high-ranking judges. [S.H.] 37. **more void:** more
empty, less crowded. 41. **speed:** prosper. 42-43. **Brutus...grant:** spoken to prevent any suspicion on the
part of Lucius. 44. **commend me:** give my love and good wishes.

ACT III. SCENE I.

The time of this scene is soon after nine o'clock in the morning of the fatal Ides of March. Shakespeare has
shifted the scene of the murder from the *curia Pompei* in the Campus Martius to the Capitol. 3. **schedule:**
document, paper. 8. **us ourself:** Caesar uses, almost unconsciously, the royal *we,* though he has not yet
received the crown.—**last serv'd:** last attended to. A splendid assumption of disinterestedness.

ART.    Delay not, Caesar! Read it instantly!

CAES.    What, is the fellow mad?

PUB.                              Sirrah, give place.                    10

CASS.    What, urge you your petitions in the street?
Come to the Capitol.

[Caesar *enters the Capitol, the rest following.*]

POP.    I wish your enterprise today may thrive.

CASS.    What enterprise, Popilius?

POP.                              Fare you well.      [*Advances to* Caesar.]

BRU.    What said Popilius Lena?                                         15

CASS.    He wish'd today our enterprise might thrive.
I fear our purpose is discovered.

BRU.    Look how he makes to Caesar. Mark him.

CASS.    Casca, be sudden, for we fear prevention.
Brutus, what shall be done? If this be known,             20
Cassius or Caesar never shall turn back,
For I will slay myself.

BRU.                              Cassius, be constant.
Popilius Lena speaks not of our purposes;
For look, he smiles, and Caesar doth not change.

CASS.    Trebonius knows his time; for look you, Brutus,          25
He draws Mark Antony out of the way.
[*Exeunt* Antony *and* Trebonius.]

DEC.    Where is Metellus Cimber? Let him go
And presently prefer his suit to Caesar.

BRU.    He is address'd. Press near and second him.

CIN.    Casca, you are the first that rears your hand.                30

CAES.    Are we all ready? What is now amiss
That Caesar and his Senate must redress?

MET.    Most high, most mighty, and most puissant Caesar,
Metellus Cimber throws before thy seat
An humble heart.                              [*Kneels.*]

---

10. **Sirrah:** a form of *sir*: used in familiar address, sometimes in contempt or reproof, often in speaking to a servant or inferior or (in more or less jocose affection) to a child. 18. **makes to:** makes up to, approaches. 19. **sudden:** prompt. There is no implication of abruptness, as in the modern use of the word.—**we fear prevention:** we fear that we may be headed off. 21. **turn back:** return to his home. 22. **be constant:** be calm, do not lose your nerve. 24. **change:** change countenance. 28. **presently:** at once, immediately.— **prefer his suit:** present his petition. 29. **address'd:** ready. 33. **puissant:** powerful.

CAES.                 I must prevent thee, Cimber.†       35
          These couchings and these lowly courtesies
          Might fire the blood of ordinary men
          And turn preordinance and first decree
          Into the law of children. Be not fond
          To think that Caesar bears such rebel blood       40
          That will be thaw'd from the true quality
          With that which melteth fools—I mean, sweet words,
          Low-crooked curtsies, and base spaniel fawning.
          Thy brother by decree is banished.
          If thou dost bend and pray and fawn for him,       45
          I spurn thee like a cur out of my way.
          Know, Caesar doth not wrong, nor without cause
          Will he be satisfied.

MET.            Is there no voice more worthy than my own,
          To sound more sweetly in great Caesar's ear       50
          For the repealing of my banish'd brother?

BRU.            I kiss thy hand, but not in flattery, Caesar,
          Desiring thee that Publius Cimber may
          Have an immediate freedom of repeal.

CAES.           What, Brutus?

CASS.                Pardon, Caesar! Caesar, pardon!       55
          As low as to thy foot doth Cassius fall
          To beg enfranchisement for Publius Cimber.

CAES.           I could be well mov'd, if I were as you;
          If I could pray to move, prayers would move me:

---

35. **prevent:** forestall, check. 36. **couchings:** crouchings, prostrations. 37. **fire the blood:** anger, incite. [S.H.] 38. **preordinance and first decree:** settled purpose and decision already made. 39-40. **the law of children:** fickleness and change. —**fond To think:** so foolish as to think.—**bears:** has.—**rebel blood:** a disposition which, on every impluse, rebels against the reason; a fickle or inconstant disposition. 41. **the true quality:** the quality or nature that it ought to have, i.e., firmness, stability. 43. **base spaniel fawning:** fawning like a dog, an obsequious gesture. [S.H.] 46. **spurn:** kick violently.—**cur:** contemptuous term for a dog [S.H.] 51. **repealing:** recall (from exile). 52. **not in flattery:** but as a personal friend. 54. **freedom of repeal:** permission to be recalled—to return from banishment. 57. **enfranchisement:** restoration of liberty. [S.H.] 58. **well:** very likely. 59. **pray to move:** beg others to change their minds. [S.H.]

---

†     During this exchange between Caesar and the senators, Bradley's film oscillates between low-angle close shots of Caesar sitting majestically in his chair and high-angle *ensemble* shots showing the isolated chair being progressively encircled from behind. The sequence thus offers two views of Caesar at the same time—a powerful one and a vulnerable one. Bradley plays on suspense and dramatic irony, Julius Caesar being unaware of the plot despite his supremacy. Mankiewicz's version makes us share Caesar's mighty vision with semi-subjective, high-angle shots of Cimber kneeling and pleading for his brother. In Burge's film, the tension is built through the atonal music and the conspirators' discreet looks at one another. [S.H.]

But I am constant as the Northern Star,                          60
Of whose true-fix'd and resting quality
There is no fellow in the firmament.
The skies are painted with unnumb'red sparks,
They are all fire, and every one doth shine;
But there's but one in all doth hold his place.                  65
So in the world: 'Tis furnish'd well with men,
And men are flesh and blood, and apprehensive;
Yet in the number I do know but one
That unassailable holds on his rank,
Unshak'd of motion; and that I am he,                            70
Let me a little show it, even in this—
That I was constant Cimber should be banish'd
And constant do remain to keep him so.

CIN.        O Caesar!

CAES.              Hence! Wilt thou lift up Olympus?

DEC.        Great Caesar!

CAES.              Doth not Brutus bootless kneel?               75

CASCA     Speak hands for me!

           *They stab* Caesar [—Casca *first,* Brutus *last*].[†]

CAES.     Et tu, Brute?—Then fall Caesar!                    *Dies.*

---

60. **Northern Star:** the Pole Star, which does not change position in the sky. [S.H.] 61. **resting quality:** immovable nature, stability. 63. **unnumb'red:** numerous, countless. [S.H.] 65. **doth hold:** which doth hold. 67. **apprehensive:** capable of perception. [S.H.] 69. **holds on his rank:** maintains his stately course. 70. **Unshak'd of motion:** unshaken either by his own impulses or by external influence. 71. **even in this:** in this small point. 72. **constant:** firm, resolute. 74. **Olympus:** the mountain (in Thessaly) home of the Greek gods. [S.H.] 75. **bootless:** in vain, uselessly. 76. **Speak hands:** Casca has not spoken before in the whole course of the petitioning. As a blunt old-fashioned republican, he finds "sweet words" impossible. 77. **Et tu, Brute?** Latin for "Even thou, Brutus?" See Introduction. [S.H.]

---

†     In Bradley's film, the murder is seen from above, the audience being thus distanced from the action. Caesar staggers from one conspirators to another, being stabbed once more each time. The film cuts to close-ups once Caesar stretches a pleading hand toward Brutus, stressing the personal betrayal when Brutus finally stabs in his turn. Under Mankiewicz's direction, the murder is no longer the focus of attention. The camera quickly concentrates on Brutus, who is looking in horror at the scene. The focal point is, therefore, no more the action but the reaction to it. Brutus is both afraid and stunned, backing away as the camera tracks toward him. The film insists on his dilemma when he closes his eyes, as if in shame, before stabbing the pleading Caesar. Burge's version, by contrast, turns the killing into a real act of butchery, focusing on wounded Caesar in close-up. The spectators are given to share Caesar's subjective vision, as everything wobbles and becomes blurred. Brutus is seen from behind while atonal music imitates the beating of Caesar's wounded heart. Suddenly, the music stops and Brutus turns back, drawing out his sword and stabbing Caesar. The bloody and cruel aspect of the assassination is emphasized once more as Caesar is injured again and again by the rest of the conspirators in a frantically-edited moment. [S.H.]

| | |
|---|---|
| Cin. | Liberty! Freedom! Tyranny is dead! |
| | Run hence, proclaim, cry it about the streets! |
| Cass. | Some to the common pulpits and cry out          80 |
| | 'Liberty, freedom, and enfranchisement!' |
| Bru. | People and Senators, be not affrighted. |
| | Fly not; stand still. Ambition's debt is paid. |
| Casca | Go to the pulpit, Brutus. |
| Dec. | And Cassius too. |
| Bru. | Where's Publius?          85 |
| Cin. | Here, quite confounded with this mutiny. |
| Met. | Stand fast together, lest some friend of Caesar's |
| | Should chance— |
| Bru. | Talk not of standing! Publius, good cheer. |
| | There is no harm intended to your person          90 |
| | Nor to no Roman else. So tell them, Publius. |
| Cass. | And leave us, Publius, lest that the people, |
| | Rushing on us, should do your age some mischief. |
| Bru. | Do so; and let no man abide this deed |
| | But we the doers. |

*Enter* Trebonius.

| | |
|---|---|
| Cass. | Where is Antony?          95 |
| Treb. | Fled to his house amaz'd. |
| | Men, wives, and children stare, cry out, and run, |
| | As it were doomsday. |
| Bru. | Fates, we will know your pleasures. |
| | That we shall die, we know; 'tis but the time, |
| | And drawing days out, that men stand upon.          100 |
| Cass. | Why, he that cuts off twenty years of life |
| | Cuts off so many years of fearing death. |
| Bru. | Grant that, and then is death a benefit. |
| | So are we Caesar's friends, that have abridg'd |

---

80. **the common pulpits:** stages for public speeches. [S.H.]  83. **Ambition's debt:** what was due to ambition. Caesar's ambition has received its deserts; no other lives are sought. 86. **mutiny:** uproar, rebellion. [S.H.] 91. **Nor…no:** an instance of the common double negative. 93. **your age:** your aged self. 94. **abide this deed:** pay for this deed, stand the consequences of this deed. 96. **amaz'd:** not merely "surprised" or "astonished" in the modern sense but "utterly confounded," "stupefied." 98. **As:** as if.—**pleasures:** the modern idiom would require the singular; the plural is used because *Fates* is plural. 100. **drawing days out:** prolonging life.—**stand upon:** insist upon—hence, attach importance to, make a point of.

|        | His time of fearing death. Stoop, Romans, stoop,      | 105 |

His time of fearing death. Stoop, Romans, stoop,                                    105
And let us bathe our hands in Caesar's blood
Up to the elbows and besmear our swords.†
Then walk we forth, even to the market place,
And waving our red weapons o'er our heads,
Let's all cry 'Peace, freedom, and liberty!'                                        110

CASS.   Stoop then and wash. How many ages hence
Shall this our lofty scene be acted over
In states unborn and accents yet unknown!

BRU.    How many times shall Caesar bleed in sport,
That now on Pompey's basis lies along                                               115
No worthier than the dust!

CASS.                                    So oft as that shall be,
So often shall the knot of us be call'd
The men that gave their country liberty.

DEC.    What, shall we forth?

CASS.                                    Ay, every man away.
Brutus shall lead, and we will grace his heels                                      120
With the most boldest and best hearts of Rome.

                                *Enter a* Servant.

BRU.    Soft! who comes here? A friend of Antony's.

---

108. **the market place:** the Forum, which was the center of Roman business and public life. 109. **red weapons:** "Brutus and his consorts, hauing their swordes bloudy in their handes, went straight to the Capitoll, perswading the Romaines as they went, to take their libertie again" (North's Plutarch). 111. **wash:** soak. [S.H.] 112. **Shall this our lofty scene,** etc. The Elizabethan dramatists are fond of figures drawn from the stage. Here Cassius seems to predict the writing of the play of JULIUS CAESAR. This sentence may call attention to the unreality of the spectacle which the audience is beholding. But by speaking of plays and acting, the *dramatis personae* also appear to emphasize the idea that they themselves were real and not mere players. [S.H.] 113. **accents:** languages. [S.H.] 114. **in sport:** for entertainment. [S.H.] 115. **basis:** pedestal.—**along:** at full length, prostrate. 117. **knot:** group, band, faction. [S.H.] 120. **grace:** do honor to. *Grace his heels* means, then, "follow him in a way to honor him or do him credit." 121. **most boldest:** double comparatives and superlatives are very common. 122. **Soft!** Merely an interjection like "hold!" Its literal meaning is "slowly!"—**friend:** the use of *friend* does not throw much light on the rank of the servant, for *friend* might mean simply "adherent," "follower," "partisan"; but the character of the servant's speech shows that he is not a menial. He is rather one of those educated slaves whom wealthy Romans employed in the most important and confidential affairs. His rank as a slave, however, justifies the pronoun *thy* which Brutus used in addressing him. See 3.1.138.

---

†       Bradley's film remains suggestive as far as bloody sights are concerned. We do not see the hands soaked in blood, and when Mark Antony offers to shake the blood-spattered hands, the camera denies a sight of the actual shaking. Mankiewicz's film hides the gory aspects of the murder in the same way. By contrast, the Burge film as well as the BBC version focus on blood, lingering over the washing in Caesar's wounds and the subsequent hand-shaking with Antony. [S.H.]

| | |
|---|---|
| SERV. | Thus, Brutus, did my master bid me kneel;[†] |
| | Thus did Mark Antony bid me fall down; |
| | And being prostrate, thus he bade me say: |
| | Brutus is noble, wise, valiant, and honest; |
| | Caesar was mighty, bold, royal, and loving. |
| | Say I love Brutus and I honor him; |
| | Say I fear'd Caesar, honor'd him, and lov'd him. |
| | If Brutus will vouchsafe that Antony |
| | May safely come to him and be resolv'd |
| | How Caesar hath deserv'd to lie in death, |
| | Mark Antony shall not love Caesar dead |
| | So well as Brutus living; but will follow |
| | The fortunes and affairs of noble Brutus |
| | Thorough the hazards of this untrod state |
| | With all true faith. So says my master Antony. |

SERV.  Thus, Brutus, did my master bid me kneel;[†]
       Thus did Mark Antony bid me fall down;
       And being prostrate, thus he bade me say:                      125
       Brutus is noble, wise, valiant, and honest;
       Caesar was mighty, bold, royal, and loving.
       Say I love Brutus and I honor him;
       Say I fear'd Caesar, honor'd him, and lov'd him.
       If Brutus will vouchsafe that Antony                           130
       May safely come to him and be resolv'd
       How Caesar hath deserv'd to lie in death,
       Mark Antony shall not love Caesar dead
       So well as Brutus living; but will follow
       The fortunes and affairs of noble Brutus                      135
       Thorough the hazards of this untrod state
       With all true faith. So says my master Antony.

BRU.   Thy master is a wise and valiant Roman.
       I never thought him worse.
       Tell him, so please him come unto this place,                 140
       He shall be satisfied and, by my honor,
       Depart untouch'd.

SERV.            I'll fetch him presently.          *Exit.*

BRU.   I know that we shall have him well to friend.

CASS.  I wish we may. But yet have I a mind
       That fears him much; and my misgiving still                   145
       Falls shrewdly to the purpose.

                    *Enter* Antony.

BRU.   But here comes Antony. Welcome, Mark Antony.[‡]

---

**126. honest:** honorable. **131. be resolv'd:** have his doubts cleared up, receive an explanation. **136. Thorough:** simply a dissyllabic pronunciation of *through.*—**this untrod state:** this novel or untried condition of the commonwealth. **140. so please him come:** if it please him to come. **141. He shall be satisfied:** he shall have full information. **142. presently:** immediately, without delay. **143. to friend:** for a friend, as a friend. **145-146. my misgiving…purpose:** When I have misgivings, they always prove to be unpleasantly near the truth. Cassius is still unconvinced as to Antony's harmlessness.

---

† In the BBC version, the Servant not only kneels but lies face down on the ground, in a sign of total submission. [S.H.]

‡ In all screen versions, Mark Antony walks past Brutus and the other conspirators without responding to their greeting, and finds his way directly to Caesar's corpse. This is most striking in Mankiewicz's film as Antony (played by Marlon Brando) advances slowly and silently through a corridor toward the camera, only to walk past the faction with a look of absolute disdain. Antony's speech can then alternate between voice-over and loud voice. In Bradley's film, this alternation is meant to preserve the intimacy of some of Antony's thoughts. In Mankiewicz's, the lines are uttered aloud, as if Antony was strong and confident enough to express himself without fear. [S.H.]

ANT.     O mighty Caesar! dost thou lie so low?
         Are all thy conquests, glories, triumphs, spoils,
         Shrunk to this little measure? Fare thee well.                    150
         I know not, gentlemen, what you intend,
         Who else must be let blood, who else is rank.
         If I myself, there is no hour so fit
         As Caesar's death's hour; nor no instrument
         Of half that worth as those your swords, made rich                155
         With the most noble blood of all this world.
         I do beseech ye, if you bear me hard,
         Now, whilst your purpled hands do reek and smoke,
         Fulfil your pleasure. Live a thousand years,
         I shall not find myself so apt to die;                            160
         No place will please me so, no mean of death,
         As here by Caesar, and by you cut off,
         The choice and master spirits of this age.

BRU.     O Antony, beg not your death of us!
         Though now we must appear bloody and cruel,                       165
         As by our hands and this our present act
         You see we do, yet see you but our hands
         And this the bleeding business they have done.
         Our hearts you see not. They are pitiful;
         And pity to the general wrong of Rome                             170
         (As fire drives out fire, so pity pity)
         Hath done this deed on Caesar. For your part,
         To you our swords have leaden points, Mark Antony.
         Our arms in strength of malice, and our hearts
         Of brothers' temper, do receive you in                           175
         With all kind love, good thoughts, and reverence.

CASS.    Your voice shall be as strong as any man's
         In the disposing of new dignities.

BRU.     Only be patient till we have appeas'd
         The multitude, beside themselves with fear,                      180

---

148. **O mighty Caesar!** Ignoring the greeting of Brutus, Antony begins at once his passionate address to the dead Caesar. 152. **must be let blood:** must be killed. [S.H.]—**rank:** too luxuriant, overgrown in power. "Who else may be supposed to have *overtopped* his equals, and *grown too high* for the publick safety?" (Samuel Johnson). 157. **bear me hard:** bear a grudge against me, are at enmity with me. 158. **purpled:** dyed crimson. 159. **Live:** the subjunctive in the conditional use: "let me live," i.e., "if I live." 160. **apt:** ready. 161. **mean:** means. 162. **by Caesar, and by you cut off:** no place to die will please me so well as here by Caesar, and no means of death so well as being cut off by you. 171. **As fire drives out fire, so pity pity:** a common proverb. Pity for the general wrong done to Rome drove out pity for Caesar. [S.H.] 173. **leaden:** blunt, heavy (suggesting that swords have been lowered). [S.H.] 174-175. **Our arms...receive you in:** Our arms, violent in enmity as they seem, and our hearts, which cherish brotherly feelings toward you, receive you in. *Malice* means simply "enmity." 177. **voice:** vote. [S.H.] 178. **dignities:** state offices. [S.H.]

|       | And then we will deliver you the cause |
|-------|----------------------------------------|
|       | Why I, that did love Caesar when I struck him, |
|       | Have thus proceeded. |
| ANT.  | I doubt not of your wisdom. |
|       | Let each man render me his bloody hand. |

First, Marcus Brutus, will I shake with you;                    185
Next, Caius Cassius, do I take your hand;
Now, Decius Brutus, yours; now yours, Metellus;
Yours, Cinna; and, my valiant Casca, yours.
Though last, not least in love, yours, good Trebonius.
Gentlemen all—Alas, what shall I say?                          190
My credit now stands on such slippery ground
That one of two bad ways you must conceit me,
Either a coward or a flatterer.
That I did love thee, Caesar, O, 'tis true!
If then thy spirit look upon us now,                           195
Shall it not grieve thee dearer than thy death
To see thy Antony making his peace,
Shaking the bloody fingers of thy foes,
Most noble! in the presence of thy corse?
Had I as many eyes as thou hast wounds,†                       200
Weeping as fast as they stream forth thy blood,
It would become me better than to close
In terms of friendship with thine enemies.
Pardon me, Julius! Here wast thou bay'd, brave hart;
Here didst thou fall; and here thy hunters stand,              205
Sign'd in thy spoil, and crimson'd in thy lethe.
O world, thou wast the forest to this hart;
And this indeed, O world, the heart of thee!
How like a deer, stroken by many princes,
Dost thou here lie!                                            210

CASS.    Mark Antony—

---

181. **deliver:** report. 191. **credit:** reputation. 192. **conceit me:** conceive me, regard me. 196. **dearer:** more keenly. 199. **corse:** corpse. [S.H.] 202. **close:** come to terms. 204. **bay'd:** brought to bay (like an animal cornered by hunters or predators). [S.H.] 206. **Sign'd in thy spoil:** marked with the signs of thy destruction. 206. **lethe:** death. Lethe was a river in Hades, to drink of which caused forgetfulness of this life. Hence its name is common as a synonym for "oblivion." 207-208. **this hart...heart of thee:** this pun no Elizabethan author could withstand. "Hart" is a deer. 209. **stroken:** struck down.

---

† As Antony delivers these lines in Mankiewicz's movie, the camera adopts the point of view of the corpse lying on the ground. In this shot, it is as if Antony's words offer a new life to the dead dictator. [S.H.]

ANT.                          Pardon me, Caius Cassius.
        The enemies of Caesar shall say this;
        Then, in a friend, it is cold modesty.

CASS.   I blame you not for praising Caesar so;
        But what compact mean you to have with us?                    215
        Will you be prick'd in number of our friends,
        Or shall we on, and not depend on you?

ANT.    Therefore I took your hands; but was indeed
        Sway'd from the point by looking down on Caesar.
        Friends am I with you all, and love you all,                  220
        Upon this hope, that you shall give me reasons
        Why and wherein Caesar was dangerous.

BRU.    Or else were this a savage spectacle.
        Our reasons are so full of good regard
        That were you, Antony, the son of Caesar,                     225
        You should be satisfied.

ANT.                            That's all I seek;
        And am moreover suitor that I may
        Produce his body to the market place
        And in the pulpit, as becomes a friend,
        Speak in the order of his funeral.                            230

BRU.    You shall, Mark Antony,

CASS.                            Brutus, a word with you.
        [*Aside to* Brutus] You know not what you do. Do not consent
        That Antony speak in his funeral.
        Know you how much the people may be mov'd
        By that which he will utter?†

BRU.    [*aside to* Cassius]            By your pardon—              235
        I will myself into the pulpit first

---

212. **shall say:** will inevitably say, must say. 213. **cold modesty:** calm moderation of language. 215. **compact:** agreement. [S.H.] 216. **prick'd:** marked, numbered, counted. It was customary to check off names or items in a list by making a little puncture in the paper or parchment with a pin or stylus, or by making a dot with a pen or pencil. 217. **shall we on?** Shall we proceed? 218. **Therefore,** etc. It was for *that* reason that I took your hands. 221. **Upon this hope:** in consequence of this hope. 224. **so full of good regard:** so well-provided with weighty considerations, so well-considered and convincing. 228. **Produce:** in the literal Latin sense, "bring forward." 230. **in the order of his funeral:** in the course of his funeral ceremonies.

---

†    This argument between Cassius and Brutus over Antony is made visually explicit in Bradley's film. A shot shows, in the foreground, Cassius on the right side of the frame and Brutus on the left, both in profile. In the background, between the two characters, Mark Antony is standing, listening intently. The object of the quarrel symbolically divides Brutus and Cassius in the structure of the shot. [S.H.]

And show the reason of our Caesar's death.
What Antony shall speak, I will protest
He speaks by leave and by permission;
And that we are contented Caesar shall                         240
Have all true rites and lawful ceremonies.
It shall advantage more than do us wrong.

CASS.     [*aside to* Brutus] I know not what may fall. I like it not.

BRU.     Mark Antony, here, take you Caesar's body.
You shall not in your funeral speech blame us,                 245
But speak all good you can devise of Caesar;
And say you do't by our permission.
Else shall you not have any hand at all
About his funeral. And you shall speak
In the same pulpit whereto I am going,                         250
After my speech is ended.

ANT.                  Be it so.
I do desire no more.

BRU.     Prepare the body then, and follow us.    *Exeunt. Manet* Antony.

ANT.     O, pardon me, thou bleeding piece of earth,
That I am meek and gentle with these butchers!                 255
Thou art the ruins of the noblest man
That ever lived in the tide of times.
Woe to the hand that shed this costly blood!
Over thy wounds now do I prophesy
(Which, like dumb mouths, do ope their ruby lips               260
To beg the voice and utterance of my tongue),
A curse shall light upon the limbs of men;
Domestic fury and fierce civil strife
Shall cumber all the parts of Italy;
Blood and destruction shall be so in use                       265
And dreadful objects so familiar
That mothers shall but smile when they behold
Their infants quartered with the hands of war,
All pity chok'd with custom of fell deeds;

---

238. **protest:** declare. 241. **true:** due and proper. 242. **advantage:** benefit.—**do us wrong:** injure us. 243. **fall:** befall, happen.—**I like it not:** Cassius is, throughout the play, overborne by the stronger will of Brutus. Cf. 2.1.113 ff., 150, 162 ff.; 4.2.37 ff.; 4.3.1 ff., 203 ff. 257. **the tide of times:** the course of the ages. 260. **like dumb mouths:** the comparison of wounds to open mouths is common. 262. **A curse...men:** men shall feel in every limb the curse that shall descend to punish what the hands of the conspirators have done. The use of *limbs* is suggested by that of *hand* in line 258. Not only shall the hands of the murderers be smitten with the curse, but all men's limbs shall share in the punishment. 264. **cumber:** burden, oppress. 266. **objects:** sights. *Object* was used for "everything that meets the eye at a single glance." 269. **fell:** savage, cruel.

"let slip the dogs of war," (3.1.273). Antony near Caesar's bloody corpse in the 1979 BBC version.

And Caesar's spirit, ranging for revenge,                           270
With Ate by his side come hot from hell,
Shall in these confines with a monarch's voice
Cry 'Havoc!' and let slip the dogs of war,
That this foul deed shall smell above the earth
With carrion men, groaning for burial.†                            275

*Enter* Octavius' Servant.
You serve Octavius Caesar, do you not?

SERV.        I do, Mark Antony.

---

270. **ranging:** roaming up and down like a wild beast in search of prey. Here Antony distinctly prophesies the survival of Caesar's influence after death and its effect in exacting vengeance from the murderers. Shakespeare has in mind the ghost of Caesar that is to appear to Brutus (4.3.275). See Introduction (pp. viii-ix). 271-272. **Ate:** goddess of discord and vengeance. Ate was a familiar figure on the Elizabethan stage.—**confines:** regions (with a sense of confined space). [S.H.] 273. **Havoc:** the cry equivalent to "No quarter!" It was used to proclaim general slaughter and pillage.—**let slip:** unleash. [S.H.] 274. **That:** so that. 276. **You serve:** the servant is obviously of a rank similar to Mark Antony's servant. See note on 3.1.122.

---

†   In Bradley's film, Antony (Charlton Heston) delivers the start of this monologue in voice-over but speaks out the prediction in a loud voice, as if the vocal delivery of the prophetic words gave them a possibility to be fulfilled. At the end of his soliloquy, he walks quickly toward the camera, almost looking at it in a threatening way. He then destroys a small copper eagle (a symbol of the Roman republic as well as Caesar's rule), thus making clear that the Roman empire as a whole will now suffer. In the Burge film, Antony (again played by Heston) delivers the whole soliloquy aloud as a promise made to Caesar, whose lifeless arm he is holding. In the BBC version, all the soliloquy is performed in voice-over except for the final exclamation starting with "Havoc!," which creates a fearful shock when it is uttered in a very loud voice. [S.H.]

| Ant. | Caesar did write for him to come to Rome. | |
|---|---|---|
| Serv. | He did receive his letters and is coming,<br>And bid me say to you by word of mouth—<br>O Caesar! | 280 |
| Ant. | Thy heart is big. Get thee apart and weep.<br>Passion, I see, is catching; for mine eyes,<br>Seeing those beads of sorrow stand in thine,<br>Began to water. Is thy master coming? | 285 |
| Serv. | He lies tonight within seven leagues of Rome. | |
| Ant. | Post back with speed and tell him what hath chanc'd.<br>Here is a mourning Rome, a dangerous Rome,<br>No Rome of safety for Octavius yet.<br>Hie hence and tell him so. Yet stay awhile.<br>Thou shalt not back till I have borne this corse<br>Into the market place. There shall I try<br>In my oration how the people take<br>The cruel issue of these bloody men;<br>According to the which thou shalt discourse<br>To young Octavius of the state of things.<br>Lend me your hand.                    *Exeunt [with* Caesar's *body].* | 290<br><br><br><br>295 |

## Scene II. [*Rome. The Forum.*]

*Enter* Brutus *and* Cassius, *with the* Plebeians.

| Plebeians | We will be satisfied! Let us be satisfied! | |
|---|---|---|
| Bru. | Then follow me and give me audience, friends.<br>Cassius, go you into the other street<br>And part the numbers.<br>Those that will hear me speak, let 'em stay here;<br>Those that will follow Cassius, go with him; | <br><br><br>5 |

---

282. **big:** swelling with grief. 283. **Passion:** grief—especially, passionate grief. 286. **lies:** lodges, is encamped. As a matter of fact, Octavius was in Illyria and did not reach Rome for about six weeks. Shakespeare, for dramatic purposes, hastens his arrival and invents the incident of a letter from Julius Caesar (278) to account for his being so near the city. 286. **seven leagues:** about 20 miles or 35 kilometers. [S.H.] 287. **Post:** ride. [S.H.]—**chanc'd:** happened. [S.H.] 289. **No Rome of safety:** an obvious pun, *Rome* being pronounced like *room*. Cf. 1.2.156: "Now is it Rome indeed, and room enough." 290. **Hie:** go quickly. [S.H.] 294. **The cruel issue of these bloody men:** the cruel deed resulting from their savage nature. *Issue* is common in the sense of "progeny" and also of "result." 295. **According to the which:** according to the way in which people take the death of Caesar.—**discourse:** describe. [S.H.]

**Scene II.**

1. **satisfied:** fully informed. 4. **part the numbers:** divide the crowd. [S.H.]

And public reasons shall be rendered
Of Caesar's death.

1. Pleb.                    I will hear Brutus speak.

2. Pleb.    I will hear Cassius, and compare their reasons
When severally we hear them rendered.                    10
                    [*Exit* Cassius, *with some of the* Plebeians.]
                    Brutus *goes into the pulpit.*

3. Pleb.    The noble Brutus is ascended. Silence!

Bru.    Be patient till the last.

Romans, countrymen, and lovers, hear me for my cause, and be silent, that you may hear. Believe me for mine honor, and have respect to mine honor, that you may believe. Censure me in your wisdom, and awake your senses, that you may the better judge. If there be any in this assembly, any dear friend of Caesar's, to him I say that Brutus' love to Caesar was no less than his. If then that friend demand why Brutus rose against Caesar, this is my answer: Not that I lov'd Caesar less, but that I lov'd Rome more. Had you rather Caesar were living, and die all slaves, than that Caesar were dead, to live all freemen? As Caesar lov'd me, I weep for him; as he was fortunate, I rejoice at it; as he was valiant, I honor him; but—as he was ambitious, I slew him. There is tears for his love; joy for his fortune; honor for his valour; and death for his ambition. Who is here so base that would be a bondman? If any, speak; for him have I offended. Who is here so rude that would not be a Roman? If any, speak; for him have I offended. Who is here so vile that will not love his country? If any, speak; for him have I offended. I pause for a reply.

All.                    None, Brutus, none!                    29

Bru.    Then none have I offended. I have done no more to Caesar than you shall do to Brutus. The question of his death is enroll'd in the Capitol; his glory not extenuated, wherein he was worthy; nor his offenses enforc'd, for which he suffered death.                    33

---

10. **severally:** separately. [S.H.] 12. **the last:** the conclusion of my address. 13. **Romans, countrymen,** etc. It has been remarked that in this speech Shakespeare aims to reproduce the actual style of Brutus, which, as we learn on ancient authority, was dry, abrupt, and unadorned. The fact that his oration is in prose brings out these qualities farther, and emphasizes the contrast between the diction of Brutus and the warm, fluent, and flexible style of Mark Antony.—**lovers:** dear friends. 14-15. **have respect to mine honor:** have regard to my honor, remember that I am an honorable man. —**Censure:** judge. 16. **senses:** intellectual powers. Brutus deliberately addresses the minds of his hearers, not their passions. 26. **rude:** boorish and ignorant. 30-31. **you shall do:** the permissive use of *shall* in the second person: "I will allow you to do as much to me when I offend in the same way." —**The question...enroll'd:** The whole matter of his death is on record. 32. **his glory not extenuated,** etc. "his glory not being understated nor his offenses unduly emphasized."

*Enter* Mark Antony [*and others*], *with* Caesar's *body.*†

Here comes his body, mourn'd by Mark Antony, who, though he had
no hand in his death, shall receive the benefit of his dying, a place in the
commonwealth, as which of you shall not? With this I depart, that, as
I slew my best lover for the good of Rome, I have the same dagger for
myself when it shall please my country to need my death.    38

ALL.          Live, Brutus! live, live!

1. PLEB.    Bring him with triumph home unto his house.    40

2. PLEB.    Give him a statue with his ancestors.

3. PLEB.    Let him be Caesar.

4. PLEB.                Caesar's better parts
              Shall be crown'd in Brutus.

1. PLEB.    We'll bring him to his house with shouts and clamors.

BRU.        My countrymen—

2. PLEB.                Peace! silence! Brutus speaks.    45

1. PLEB.    Peace, ho!

BRU.        Good countrymen, let me depart alone,
              And, for my sake, stay here with Antony.
              Do grace to Caesar's corpse, and grace his speech
              Tending to Caesar's glories which Mark Antony,    50
              By our permission, is allow'd to make.
              I do entreat you, not a man depart,
              Save I alone, till Antony have spoke.          *Exit.*

1. PLEB.    Stay, ho! and let us hear Mark Antony.

---

35-36. **a place in the commonwealth:** free citizenship, a citizen's place in the free state. The implication is
that in Caesar's lifetime all Romans were subjects or slaves. 41. **Give...ancestors:** in particular, with Lucius
Junius Brutus, the Liberator. 42. **Let him be Caesar:** there is unconscious irony in the citizen's cry. He
shows how little he understands free citizenship.—**parts:** qualities. 49. **Do...speech:** do respect to Caesar's
body, and honor Antony's address (by your presence). 50. **tending:** relating, dealing with. [S.H.] 53. **Save
I:** a common construction (as well as *save me*) in the Elizabethan time.

---

†    At this point of Mankiewicz's film, a shot draws attention to a woman in the crowd, blurting out
a loud scream. The audience may think at first that she is reacting to Brutus's allusion to Caesar's
death, but the following shot reveals the actual cause of her distress: Mark Antony has suddenly
come out of the Capitol, carrying Caesar's dead body. Mankiewicz here reverses the usual pattern of
the shot/countershot technique. Instead of presenting an action and then a reaction to this action,
he shows the woman's response before disclosing the event that has induced it. Here, it emphasizes
Antony's entrance, making it more spectacular and emotional. Antony is filmed with a low-angle
shot stressing his charismatic, arresting *persona*. [S.H.]

3. PLEB.    Let him go up into the public chair.                                    55
            We'll hear him. Noble Antony, go up.

ANT.        For Brutus' sake I am beholding to you.              [*Goes up.*]

4. PLEB.    What does he say of Brutus?

3. PLEB.                            He says for Brutus' sake
            He finds himself beholding to us all.

4. PLEB.    'Twere best he speak no harm of Brutus here!                          60

1. PLEB.    This Caesar was a tyrant.

3. PLEB.                            Nay, that's certain.
            We are blest that Rome is rid of him.

2. PLEB.    Peace! Let us hear what Antony can say.

ANT.        You gentle Romans—

ALL.                            Peace, ho! Let us hear him.

ANT.        Friends, Romans, countrymen, lend me your ears;†                     65
            I come to bury Caesar, not to praise him.
            The evil that men do lives after them;
            The good is oft interred with their bones.
            So let it be with Caesar. The noble Brutus
            Hath told you Caesar was ambitious.                                  70
            If it were so, it was a grievous fault,
            And grievously hath Caesar answer'd it.
            Here, under leave of Brutus and the rest
            (For Brutus is an honorable man;
            So are they all, all honorable men),                                 75
            Come I to speak in Caesar's funeral.

---

55. **the public chair:** probably no more is meant than what is elsewhere called "the pulpit." 57. **beholding:** beholden, obliged. *For Brutus' sake* implies that the mob has given Antony the favor of a patient hearing out of consideration for Brutus. 61. **a tyrant:** i.e., a *usurping* tyrant. The word commonly carried with it the idea of royal power unlawfully obtained. 64. **You gentle Romans:** gentlemen of Rome. 68. **interred:** buried. [S.H.] 72. **answer'd it:** paid for it. 73. **under leave:** with the permission of. [S.H.]

---

†    In Burge's 1970 film, editing alternatively shows the crowd and Antony (Charlton Heston), generally
     in close-shots. There are no establishing shots revealing how huge the crowd is, thus lessening the
     threatening potential of the throng. Antony starts speaking by addressing a few people near him,
     grabbing their hands and arms. Before displaying the corpse of Caesar, he takes a woman's face
     between his hands to prepare her for the shock to come. Antony remains very close to the people,
     staying physically among them. He is less a real Machiavellian than a Moses-like salvager who
     wishes to guide the Roman people towards the light of truth and justice. Mankiewicz's 1953 film, in
     contradistinction, features a highly manipulative Antony, played by Marlon Brando. The sequence
     works on a strong opposition between an impressive throng and a lonely man. In the course of the
     scene, the shift of authority from the citizens to Antony is made perceptible through changes in
     camera angles. Low-angle and high-angle shots in turns reflect the power that one side gains over the
     other. [S.H.]

Antony about to deliver his speech to the Roman citizens in Burge's 1970 film. American International Pictures / Photofest; © American International Pictures.

He was my friend, faithful and just to me;
But Brutus says he was ambitious,
And Brutus is an honorable man.
He hath brought many captives home to Rome,                    80
Whose ransoms did the general coffers fill.
Did this in Caesar seem ambitious?
When that the poor have cried, Caesar hath wept;
Ambition should be made of sterner stuff.
Yet Brutus says he was ambitious;                              85
And Brutus is an honorable man.
You all did see that on the Lupercal
I thrice presented him a kingly crown,
Which he did thrice refuse. Was this ambition?
Yet Brutus says he was ambitious;                             90
And sure he is an honorable man.
I speak not to disprove what Brutus spoke,
But here I am to speak what I do know.
You all did love him once, not without cause.
What cause withholds you then to mourn for him?              95
O judgment, thou art fled to brutish beasts,

77. **just:** exact and punctual in all the duties of friendship.

And men have lost their reason! Bear with me.
My heart is in the coffin there with Caesar,
And I must pause till it come back to me.†

1. PLEB.      Methinks there is much reason in his sayings.      100

2. PLEB.      If thou consider rightly of the matter,
Caesar has had great wrong.

3. PLEB.                    Has he, masters?
I fear there will a worse come in his place.

4. PLEB.      Mark'd ye his words? He would not take the crown;
Therefore 'tis certain he was not ambitious.      105

1. PLEB.      If it be found so, some will dear abide it.

2. PLEB.      Poor soul! his eyes are red as fire with weeping.

3. PLEB.      There's not a nobler man in Rome than Antony.

4. PLEB.      Now mark him. He begins again to speak.

ANT.      But yesterday the word of Caesar might      110
Have stood against the world. Now lies he there,
And none so poor to do him reverence.
O masters! If I were dispos'd to stir
Your hearts and minds to mutiny and rage,
I should do Brutus wrong, and Cassius wrong,      115
Who, you all know, are honorable men.
I will not do them wrong. I rather choose
To wrong the dead, to wrong myself and you,
Than I will wrong such honorable men.
But here's a parchment with the seal of Caesar.      120
I found it in his closet; 'tis his will.
Let but the commons hear this testament,

---

106. **dear abide it:** pay dear for it. 112. **to do:** as to do. 114. **mutiny:** disorder, riot. Frequently used with no suggestion of an insurrection against constituted authority. 121. **closet:** private room, study. 122. **commons:** the citizens, the people. [S.H.]

---

†     In Mankiewicz's film, Antony's supposedly emotional pause comes, in fact, as a rhetorical device to ensure that his speech is working. For the first time in the sequence, Antony is filmed in close-up, as he turns his back to the crowd. We are witnessing something that remains hidden to the crowd—Antony's cunning little smile as he glimpses behind him to check if his scheme is functioning as planned. From this moment forth, we are made certain of Antony's manipulative skills and opportunistic attitude. While he has his back turned on purpose, the leaders in the crowd discuss in echoing close-ups, approving Antony's sayings. The crowd is now aesthetically split into many smaller, less threatening groups. They are no longer filmed in low-angle shots, reflecting how the danger they represent has lessened. For the first time, they are filmed on the same level as Antony. Taming a crowd, in this film, means convincing a few leaders of opinion, who will then rally all the people behind them, herding them as if they were mere sheep. [S.H.]

|          | Which (pardon me) I do not mean to read, |     |
|----------|------------------------------------------|-----|
|          | And they would go and kiss dead Caesar's wounds | |
|          | And dip their napkins in his sacred blood; | 125 |
|          | Yea, beg a hair of him for memory, |     |
|          | And dying, mention it within their wills, | |
|          | Bequeathing it as a rich legacy |     |
|          | Unto their issue. |     |
| 4. Pleb. | We'll hear the will! Read it, Mark Antony. | 130 |
| All.     | The will, the will! We will hear Caesar's will! | |
| Ant.     | Have patience, gentle friends; I must not read it. | |
|          | It is not meet you know how Caesar lov'd you. | |
|          | You are not wood, you are not stones, but men; | |
|          | And being men, hearing the will of Caesar, | 135 |
|          | It will inflame you, it will make you mad. | |
|          | 'Tis good you know not that you are his heirs; | |
|          | For if you should, O, what would come of it? | |
| 4. Pleb. | Read the will! We'll hear it, Antony! | |
|          | You shall read us the will, Caesar's will! | 140 |
| Ant.     | Will you be patient? Will you stay awhile? | |
|          | I have o'ershot myself to tell you of it. | |
|          | I fear I wrong the honorable men | |
|          | Whose daggers have stabb'd Caesar; I do fear it. | |
| 4. Pleb. | They were traitors. Honorable men! | 145 |
| All.     | The will! the testament! | |
| 2. Pleb. | They were villains, murderers! The will! Read the will! | |
| Ant.     | You will compel me then to read the will? | |
|          | Then make a ring about the corpse of Caesar | |
|          | And let me show you him that made the will. | 150 |
|          | Shall I descend? and will you give me leave?[†] | |
| All.     | Come down. | |
| 2. Pleb. | Descend. | |

125. **napkins:** handkerchiefs. The line refers to the custom of dipping cloths in the blood of martyrs and preserving them as precious and even medicinal relics. See 2.2.89, and note. 129. **issue:** descendants. [S.H.] 133. **meet:** fitting. [S.H.] 137. Antony discloses the main fact about the will by the very words of his refusal to read it. 142. **o'ershot myself:** shot beyond the mark, gone farther than I intended. A figure from archery.

†   At this moment, in Mankiewicz's film, the camera focuses on the profile of the sightless old man who had delivered the prophecy of the Ides of March at the start of the film. This shot reminds us of the tragedy being announced and foretold from the beginning. The old man's face is directed away from the whole event as if, after being ignored, he did not feel concerned or involved any longer. [S.H.]

3. PLEB.    You shall have leave.              [Antony *comes down.*]

4. PLEB.    A ring! Stand round.                                         155

1. PLEB.    Stand from the hearse! Stand from the body!

2. PLEB.    Room for Antony, most noble Antony!

ANT.    Nay, press not so upon me. Stand far off.

ALL.    Stand back! Room! Bear back!

ANT.    If you have tears, prepare to shed them now.[†]                 160
          You all do know this mantle. I remember
          The first time ever Caesar put it on.
          'Twas on a summer's evening in his tent,
          That day he overcame the Nervii.
          Look, in this place ran Cassius' dagger through.              165
          See what a rent the envious Casca made.
          Through this the well-beloved Brutus stabb'd;
          And as he pluck'd his cursed steel away,
          Mark how the blood of Caesar followed it,
          As rushing out of doors to be resolv'd                        170
          If Brutus so unkindly knock'd or no;
          For Brutus, as you know, was Caesar's angel.
          Judge, O you gods, how dearly Caesar lov'd him!
          This was the most unkindest cut of all;
          For when the noble Caesar saw him stab,                       175
          Ingratitude, more strong than traitors' arms,
          Quite vanquish'd him. Then burst his mighty heart;
          And in his mantle muffling up his face,
          Even at the base of Pompey's statue
          (Which all the while ran blood) great Caesar fell.            180
          O, what a fall was there, my countrymen!

---

156. **the hearse:** the bier. 158. **far off:** *far* sometimes means "farther," and so, perhaps, here, though the usual sense would do well enough. 159. **Bear back!** Move back! 161. **mantle:** cloak, toga. [S.H.] 164. **the Nervii:** Caesar overcame the Nervii, a warlike tribe of Belgic Gaul, in 57 B.C., thirteen years before his death. His victory had been celebrated at Rome by an unprecedented thanksgiving. Antony was not with him in this campaign. He visited Caesar in Gaul in 54 B.C. Shakespeare uses poetic license, as always in dramatizing historical details. 166. **rent:** tear. [S.H.]—**envious:** malignant, malicious. 170. **to be resolv'd:** to have all doubts cleared up, to learn for certain. 172. **angel:** dearest friend, darling. It was in reality Decimus Brutus (Shakespeare's Decius)—not Marcus Brutus—who was a particular friend of Caesar's. 179. **base:** pedestal.

---

†    When Antony tears Caesar's toga to display his gruesome wounds to the crowd, Mankiewicz uses the same reversal of the usual action/reaction shot that he has already employed for Antony's entrance. The crowd's heartfelt reaction is filmed before the corpse itself, enhancing the horror through suggestion: we are asked to imagine the state of the body according to the people's responses before we even see it. In a slow and silent pan, the camera moves along the citizens' faces as they look upon the body in dismay and shame. It is as if the Romans were digesting Caesar's death before exploding into mutiny. [S.H.]

Then I, and you, and all of us fell down,
Whilst bloody treason flourish'd over us.
O, now you weep, and I perceive you feel
The dint of pity. These are gracious drops.           185
Kind souls, what weep you when you but behold
Our Caesar's vesture wounded? Look you here!
Here is himself, marr'd as you see with traitors.

1. PLEB.  O piteous spectacle!

2. PLEB.  O noble Caesar!                                    190

3. PLEB.  O woful day!

4. PLEB.  O traitors, villains!

1. PLEB.  O most bloody sight!

2. PLEB.  We will be reveng'd.

ALL.     Revenge! About! Seek! Burn! Fire! Kill! Slay! Let not a traitor live!  195

ANT.     Stay, countrymen.

1. PLEB.  Peace there! Hear the noble Antony.

2. PLEB.  We'll hear him, we'll follow him, we'll die with him!

ANT.     Good friends, sweet friends, let me not stir you up
         To such a sudden flood of mutiny.                  200
         They that have done this deed are honorable.
         What private griefs they have, alas, I know not,
         That made them do it. They are wise and honorable,
         And will no doubt with reasons answer you.
         I come not, friends, to steal away your hearts.     205
         I am no orator, as Brutus is,
         But (as you know me all) a plain blunt man
         That love my friend; and that they know full well
         That gave me public leave to speak of him.
         For I have neither wit, nor words, nor worth,        210
         Action, nor utterance, nor the power of speech
         To stir men's blood. I only speak right on.
         I tell you that which you yourselves do know,
         Show you sweet Caesar's wounds, poor poor dumb mouths,

183: **flourish'd:** several meanings are here conveyed: "grew rampant," "triumphed" and "brandished its sword." [S.H.] 185. **dint:** stroke.—**gracious:** either (1) honorable or (2) becoming. The sense is practically the same in either case: "tears that do credit to your good feeling and soundness of heart." 186. **what:** why. 187. **vesture:** garments. [S.H.] 200. **mutiny:** disorder, riot. 202. **griefs:** grievances. Antony artfully suggests that there can have been no public reason for the murder of Caesar, and that the conspirators were actuated by motives of private vengeance. 207. **blunt:** dull, without mental acuteness 210. **wit:** intellectual cleverness. 214. **dumb mouths:** cf. 3.1.260.

|  |  |  |
|---|---|---|
|  | And bid them speak for me. But were I Brutus, | 215 |
|  | And Brutus Antony, there were an Antony |  |
|  | Would ruffle up your spirits, and put a tongue |  |
|  | In every wound of Caesar that should move |  |
|  | The stones of Rome to rise and mutiny. |  |
| ALL. | We'll mutiny. |  |
| 1. PLEB. | We'll burn the house of Brutus. | 220 |
| 3. PLEB. | Away then! Come, seek the conspirators.† |  |
| ANT. | Yet hear me, countrymen. Yet hear me speak. |  |
| ALL. | Peace, ho! Hear Antony, most noble Antony! |  |
| ANT. | Why, friends, you go to do you know not what. |  |
|  | Wherein hath Caesar thus deserv'd your loves? | 225 |
|  | Alas, you know not! I must tell you then. |  |
|  | You have forgot the will I told you of. |  |
| ALL. | Most true! The will! Let's stay and hear the will. |  |
| ANT. | Here is the will, and under Caesar's seal. |  |
|  | To every Roman citizen he gives, | 230 |
|  | To every several man, seventy-five drachmas. |  |
| 2. PLEB. | Most noble Caesar! We'll revenge his death! |  |
| 3. PLEB. | O royal Caesar! |  |
| ANT. | Hear me with patience. |  |
| ALL. | Peace, ho! | 235 |
| ANT. | Moreover, he hath left you all his walks, |  |
|  | His private arbors, and new-planted orchards, |  |
|  | On this side Tiber; he hath left them you, |  |
|  | And to your heirs for ever—common pleasures, |  |
|  | To walk abroad and recreate yourselves. | 240 |
|  | Here was a Caesar! When comes such another? |  |
| 1. PLEB. | Never, never! Come, away, away! |  |
|  | We'll burn his body in the holy place |  |
|  | And with the brands fire the traitors' houses. |  |
|  | Take up the body. | 245 |

---

217. **ruffle up:** rouse to madness. The word was much stronger than today. A *ruffler* was a quarrelsome ruffian. 231. **drachmas:** silver coins. 237. **orchards:** gardens. 239. **pleasures:** pleasure grounds. 240. **recreate:** "entertain," but also "regenerate," "renew." [S.H.] 244. **(fire)brands:** burning wood. [S.H.]

---

†     At this point in the BBC version, the crowd moves away from Caesar's body and leaves only one man near the corpse—the Soothsayer, watching Caesar with sadness. The shot reflects on Caesar's miscalculations and lack of clairvoyance. [S.H.]

Antony having led the people to mutiny in Mankiewicz's film (3.2.246).

| 2. PLEB. | Go fetch fire! |
| 3. PLEB. | Pluck down benches! |
| 4. PLEB. | Pluck down forms, windows, anything!† |

*Exeunt* Plebeians [*with the body*].

ANT.    Now let it work. Mischief, thou art afoot,
Take thou what course thou wilt.‡

*Enter* Servant.

How now, fellow?                                    250

---

247. **pluck:** tear. [S.H.] 248. **forms:** long benches.

---

† These lines have given the film directors opportunities for some spectacular scenes of violent riots. Bradley builds an atmosphere of darkness, only broken by the fires lit by the people seen in extreme, expressionistic close-ups. Houses are burnt down, and flames invade the whole space of the screen. Burge's version shows us more realistic events in a heavily edited sequence: the people throw food out of baskets, destroy furniture, carry threatening torches and kill in the streets. Under Mankiewicz's direction, the destruction is not filmed in different shots, but presented in all its extensive scale in one establishing shot. Chaos invades the whole screen as people move everywhere; scaffolds are brought down; columns and statues are smashed. [S.H.]

‡ Film directors have generally stressed the Machiavellian and opportunistic aspect of these lines. In Bradley's film, the camera tracks toward Antony's still face while the lines are delivered in a voice-over with a very cold and detached tone, as his image invades the screen. Charlton Heston reproduces the same style of detached acting twenty years later in the Burge production, but this time in loud voice and drinking wine dispassionately. In the Mankiewicz film, only Mark Antony remains poised and impassive during the mutiny. Filmed in the foreground of the chaotic activity, he walks slowly towards us, contemplating his work and smiling ironically. This last shot in the sequence emphasizes Antony's victory over a manipulated, giddy crowd. [S.H.]

| | | |
|---|---|---|
| SERV. | Sir, Octavius is already come to Rome. | |
| ANT. | Where is he? | |
| SERV. | He and Lepidus are at Caesar's house. | |
| ANT. | And thither will I straight to visit him. | |
| | He comes upon a wish. Fortune is merry, | 255 |
| | And in this mood will give us anything. | |
| SERV. | I heard him say Brutus and Cassius | |
| | Are rid like madmen through the gates of Rome. | |
| ANT. | Belike they had some notice of the people | |
| | How I had mov'd them. Bring me to Octavius. | *Exeunt.* 260 |

### SCENE III. [*Rome. A street.*]

*Enter* Cinna *the* Poet, *and after him the* Plebeians.†

CIN.    I dreamt tonight that I did feast with Caesar,
       And things unluckily charge my fantasy.

---

251. **already come to Rome:** In the play, the orations of Brutus and Antony, Caesar's funeral, and the arrival of Octavius in Rome all take place upon the day of the assassination (March 15, 44 B.C.). In fact, the speech of Brutus in the Forum was delivered on the 16th, and on the 17th he addressed the people again in the Capitol. Only the second of these speeches was received with applause. The funeral of Caesar, with Antony's oration, came still later—not before the 19th. As for Octavius, he was in Illyria when Caesar was murdered, and did not reach Rome for about six weeks. Shakespeare has condensed history with a sure eye for dramatic effect. 253. **Lepidus:** Marcus Aemilius Lepidus, a partisan of Caesar, was outside Rome with an army at the time of the murder. In the course of the next night he entered the city with his troops and thus became a person of importance in the events that followed. 255. **upon a wish:** just when he is wanted; most opportunely. As a matter of history, Antony was not much pleased at the coming of Octavius, for he had affairs more or less under his own control.—**Fortune:** in Roman mythology, Fortuna (equivalent to the Greek goddess Tyche) was the personification of luck (hopefully of good luck) but she could be shown veiled and blind, thus representing the capriciousness of life. The Elizabethans inherited from medieval philosophy the concept of the "wheel of Fortune," again referring to the whimsical nature of Fate. [S.H.] 256. **mood:** that Fortune's mood is favorable is shown by the opportune arrival of Octavius. 258. **are rid:** have ridden. [S.H.] 259-260. **Belike:** probably.—**some notice…them:** some news how I had moved the people.—**of:** concerning.

**SCENE III.**

This scene takes place on the same day as scene 2. The incident is reported by Suetonius and Plutarch as occurring immediately after Caesar's funeral. C. Helvius Cinna was a friend of Catullus and a poet of distinction in his day. Only a few lines of his verse have survived. 1. **tonight:** last night. 2. **things… fantasy:** the events that have happened oppress my imagination with forebodings. Since "dreams go by contraries," it was thought to be unlucky to dream of feasting, and to dream of feasting *with Caesar* would be especially ominous under the circumstances.

---

†    This highly disturbing scene is entirely cut in Mankiewicz's and Burge's versions. It is, however, present in the BBC 1979 production (which offers a full-text version) and, more surprisingly, in Bradley's independent film. In the latter, the whole sequence is framed by fire to stress the cruelty and brutality of the action. Cinna the Poet is burnt and beaten up, and soon disappears under a wild and ravenous scramble. Finally, the crowd leaves him alone and dead. The camera highlights his isolation with a high-angle, detached shot. [S.H.]

|         | I have no will to wander forth of doors,                                                          |    |
|---------|---------------------------------------------------------------------------------------------------|----|
|         | Yet something leads me forth.                                                                      |    |
| 1. Pleb.| What is your name?                                                                                 | 5  |
| 2. Pleb.| Whither are you going?                                                                             |    |
| 3. Pleb.| Where do you dwell?                                                                                |    |
| 4. Pleb.| Are you a married man or a bachelor?                                                               |    |
| 2. Pleb.| Answer every man directly.                                                                         |    |
| 1. Pleb.| Ay, and briefly.                                                                                   | 10 |
| 4. Pleb.| Ay, and wisely.                                                                                    |    |
| 3. Pleb.| Ay, and truly, you were best.                                                                      |    |
| Cin.    | What is my name? Whither am I going? Where do I dwell? Am I a married man or a bachelor? Then, to answer every man directly and briefly, wisely and truly: wisely I say, I am a bachelor. | 15 |
| 2. Pleb.| That's as much as to say they are fools that marry. You'll bear me a bang for that, I fear. Proceed—directly. |    |
| Cin.    | Directly I am going to Caesar's funeral.                                                           |    |
| 1. Pleb.| As a friend or an enemy?                                                                           |    |
| Cin.    | As a friend.                                                                                       | 20 |
| 2. Pleb.| That matter is answered directly.                                                                  |    |
| 4. Pleb.| For your dwelling—briefly.                                                                         |    |
| Cin.    | Briefly, I dwell by the Capitol.                                                                   |    |
| 3. Pleb.| Your name, sir, truly.                                                                             |    |
| Cin.    | Truly, my name is Cinna.                                                                           | 25 |
| 1. Pleb.| Tear him to pieces! He's a conspirator.                                                            |    |
| Cin.    | I am Cinna the poet! I am Cinna the poet!                                                          |    |
| 4. Pleb.| Tear him for his bad verses! Tear him for his bad verses!                                          |    |
| Cin.    | I am not Cinna the conspirator.                                                                    |    |
| 4. Pleb.| It is no matter; his name's Cinna! Pluck but his name out of his heart, and turn him going. | 31 |
| 3. Pleb.| Tear him, tear him! Come, brands, ho! firebrands! To Brutus', to Cassius'! Burn all! Some to Decius' house and some to Casca's; some to Ligarius'! Away, go!                *Exeunt all the* Plebeians [*with* Cinna]. |    |

---

3. **of doors:** from doors, i.e., out of doors, from home. 9. **directly:** straightforwardly, without shuffling. Cf. 1.1.12: "What trade art thou? Answer me directly." 12. **you were best:** "It were (i.e., would be) best for you." 16. **You'll bear me a bang:** You will get a knock from me. 31. **turn him going:** send him packing. [S.H.]

# ACT IV

SCENE I. [*Rome.* Antony's *house.*]

*Enter* Antony, Octavius, *and* Lepidus.[†]

ANT. These many, then, shall die; their names are prick'd.

OCT. Your brother too must die. Consent you, Lepidus?

LEP. I do consent—

OCT.     Prick him down, Antony.

LEP. Upon condition Publius shall not live,
  Who is your sister's son, Mark Antony.      5

ANT. He shall not live. Look, with a spot I damn him.[‡]
  But, Lepidus, go you to Caesar's house.

---

**ACT IV. SCENE I.**

Antony, Octavius, and Lepidus are making a list for the proscription (the posting-up of the names of condemned persons) which marked their ascendancy at Rome after the flight of the conspirators. This meeting, at which the so-called Second Triumvirate was organized, did not in fact take place until October, 43 B.C., a year and a half after the assassination of Caesar. In the meantime there had been active hostilities between Octavius and Antony. These Shakespeare has ignored, as being of no dramatic value. The place of the meeting is a house in Rome, probably Antony's, certainly not Caesar's (lines 7-11). 1. **These many,** etc. The Triumvirs have all but finished their business of proscription when the scene opens. Antony holds the list of hostile or suspected persons and has been pricking the names on which they agree, i.e., marking them with a puncture or dot (cf. 3.1.216). The horror of the whole business comes out vividly in the indifference with which Antony sacrifices his own nephew, and Lepidus his own brother. 2. **Your brother:** Lucius Aemilius Paullus, Lepidus's elder brother, once consul and supporter of Brutus. [S.H.] 5. **sister's son:** Antony had no nephew Publius. His uncle Lucius Caesar (his mother's brother) was among those proscribed, as Shakespeare must have known from Plutarch. There is no telling whether the dramatist made a mistake here, or whether his departure from history is intentional. Both the brother of Lepidus and Antony's uncle were finally spared. 6. **He shall not live…him:** it is not Shakespeare's purpose that we should take sides with the Triumvirs, and he thus, by a mere touch, alienates the sympathy and admiration which we may have acquired for Antony in the preceding act.—**damn:** condemn, doom.

---

[†] Bradley's film offers an interesting transition from the murder of Cinna to the Proscription scene. Images of fire and destruction slowly dissolves into a shot of a candle on the table at which Lepidus, Octavius and Antony are sitting. The film subtly shows how the popular riots are going to be politically appropriated by the future Triumvirate. At the end of the Proscription scene, the same kind of transition will occur as we move from the candle to torches at the military camp in Sardis. Through those dissolves, Bradley's film shows the link between the riots, their political use and the civil war. [S.H.]

[‡] In Bradley's version, Antony casually erases Publius's name with a drop of wine, thus stressing the contrast between the relaxed situation of the meeting and the definitive and ruthless actions that are decided. In Burge's version, the scene takes place in a steam house where Antony and Octavius are being massaged. By contrast, Lepidus is standing between them, fully clothed. Burge's direction thus creates a distinct separation between Antony and Octavius on one side, reveling in their strength and virility, and Lepidus on the other, who is soon sent away and mocked. [S.H.]

Fetch the will hither, and we shall determine
How to cut off some charge in legacies.

LEP.    What? shall I find you here?                              10

OCT.    Or here or at the Capitol.              *Exit* Lepidus.

ANT.    This is a slight unmeritable man,
        Meet to be sent on errands. Is it fit,
        The threefold world divided, he should stand
        One of the three to share it?

OCT.                         So you thought him,                  15
        And took his voice who should be prick'd to die
        In our black sentence and proscription.

ANT.    Octavius, I have seen more days than you;
        And though we lay these honors on this man
        To ease ourselves of divers sland'rous loads,           20
        He shall but bear them as the ass bears gold,
        To groan and sweat under the business,
        Either led or driven as we point the way;
        And having brought our treasure where we will,
        Then take we down his load, and turn him off            25
        (Like to the empty ass) to shake his ears
        And graze in commons.

OCT.                         You may do your will;
        But he's a tried and valiant soldier.

ANT.    So is my horse, Octavius, and for that
        I do appoint him store of provender.                    30
        It is a creature that I teach to fight,
        To wind, to stop, to run directly on,
        His corporal motion govern'd by my spirit.
        And, in some taste, is Lepidus but so.

---

9. **cut off some charge:** abridge some expenditure. 12. **slight unmeritable:** of slight account, and undeserving. 14. **The threefold world divided:** It was the intention of the Triumvirs to parcel out the Roman Empire among themselves.—**threefold:** with reference to Europe, Asia, and Africa. Antony governed Gaul, Lepidus governed Spain, and Octavius governed Africa, Sardinia and Sicily. [S.H.]—**stand:** practically equivalent to *be.* 16. **took his voice:** "asked for his opinion" or "accepted his decision." [S.H.] 17. **proscription:** a statute devised by the triumvirate to declare their enemies traitors and seize their property. [S.H.] 20. **divers sland'rous loads:** many sorts of burdens of blame. [S.H.] 26. **empty:** without his precious load.—**to shake his ears:** a common expression equivalent to "act uselessly or aimlessly." 27. **in commons:** Common lands for pasturage were, in Shakespeare's day, adjacent to most villages, and the horse or donkey out of work and grazing on what he could find there was a familiar figure. 28. **soldier:** Lepidus had shown his prompt soldiership by bringing troops into the city and taking possession of the Forum during the night that followed the murder. 30. **appoint:** assign, allot.—**store of provender:** supply of fodder. 32. **to wind:** to turn. [S.H.] 33. **corporal:** bodily.—**spirit:** mind. 34. **in some taste:** to some extent, in some degree.

He must be taught, and train'd, and bid go forth:           35
A barren-spirited fellow; one that feeds
On objects, arts, and imitations
Which, out of use and stal'd by other men
Begin his fashion. Do not talk of him,
But as a property. And now, Octavius,                       40
Listen great things. Brutus and Cassius
Are levying powers. We must straight make head.
Therefore let our alliance be combin'd,
Our best friends made, our means stretch'd;
And let us presently go sit in council                      45
How covert matters may be best disclos'd
And open perils surest answered.

OCT.     Let us do so; for we are at the stake
And bay'd about with many enemies;
And some that smile have in their hearts, I fear,
Millions of mischiefs.                      *Exeunt.*[†]

---

36. **barren-spirited:** of unproductive mind, without ideas of his own. What follows carries out the thought: he has no ideas, he can originate nothing; his utmost is to follow other men's ideas. 37. **On objects, arts,** etc. The point is that all the *objects* that busy Lepidus, all the *arts* of life which he practices, and even all the *imitations* (the mere *fashions*) which he undertakes to copy in his turn, are such as have long ago lost their freshness and interest for other people. He is a tardy copyist of other men, not only in their *objects* and *arts* but even in their *imitations.* 39. **Begin:** Lepidus comes into a fashion intellectually when other people go out. 40. **a property:** a thing, or utensil; a mere tool, as opposed to "a person." In the language of the theater, tables, chairs, candlesticks, and other movable articles used in fitting out the stage but not of the nature of scenery are called now, as they were in Shakespeare's time, *properties.* Lepidus is not fit to be an actor in the great drama that is going on; he can simply be one of the lifeless things used by the real actors (Antony and Octavius) in playing their parts. 42. **make head:** collect an armed force. 44. **made:** collected, mustered.—**stretch'd:** extended or used to the utmost, made to go as far as possible. 45. **presently:** without delay. 46-47. **disclos'd:** discovered. *Covert matters* is opposed to *open perils.*—**answered:** met, encountered. 48. **we are at the stake:** the figure comes from the favorite Elizabethan sport of bear-baiting. They are like the bear chained to his stake. The dogs are barking about them, eager for the attack, but still on the leash.

---

†    Mankiewicz gives a very dramatic turn to the end of the Proscription scene. Lepidus and Octavius gone, Antony remains alone in Caesar's former house. He walks to Caesar's bust and turns the statue toward his face. In this move, Antony bends Caesar to his will and replaces him as the new imperial figure. History repeats itself as we are made to understand that the same kind of mighty, unilateral power will rule over Rome. With the same musical theme that accompanied Caesar's triumph at the start of the movie, Antony finally sits in Caesar's sumptuous chair on which the imperial eagle can clearly be seen. [S.H.]

SCENE II. [*The camp near Sardis. Before the tent of* Brutus.]

*Drum. Enter* Brutus, Lucilius, Lucius, *and the* Army.
Titinius *and* Pindarus *meet them.*

BRU.        Stand ho!

LUCIL.      Give the word, ho! and stand!

BRU.        What now, Lucilius? Is Cassius near?

LUCIL.      He is at hand, and Pindarus is come
            To do you salutation from his master.                    5

BRU.        He greets me well. Your master, Pindarus,
            In his own change, or by ill officers,
            Hath given me some worthy cause to wish
            Things done undone; but if he be at hand,
            I shall be satisfied.

PIN.                    I do not doubt                                10
            But that my noble master will appear
            Such as he is, full of regard and honor.

BRU.        He is not doubted. A word, Lucilius,
            How he receiv'd you. Let me be resolv'd.

LUCIL.      With courtesy and with respect enough,                   15
            But not with such familiar instances
            Nor with such free and friendly conference
            As he hath us'd of old.

BRU.                    Thou hast describ'd
            A hot friend cooling. Ever note, Lucilius,
            When love begins to sicken and decay                     20
            It useth an enforced ceremony.
            There are no tricks in plain and simple faith;

**SCENE II.**

The time of this and the following scene (which take place on the same day) is not long after that of scene 1, for Brutus and Messala have just received word of the proscription (4.3.167-180). In the interval, Antony and Octavius have collected large forces and are marching toward Philippi, where they hope to encounter Brutus and Cassius (5.1.1-6). 6. **He greets me well:** a gracious compliment to this trusted slave: "Cassius has sent his salutation by a man from whom I am glad to receive it." 7. **In his own change... officers:** whether from a change in his own feelings toward me or because of the acts of untrustworthy subordinates. 8. **worthy:** substantial. 9. **undone:** not done. 10. **I shall be satisfied:** I shall doubtless receive a full explanation. 11-12. **will appear...honor:** when you talk with him, you will find that he has acted with due regard both to your wishes and to his own honor. 14. **be resolv'd:** have my doubts cleared up, be fully informed. 15. **respect:** attention. 16. **familiar instances:** proofs or marks of intimate friendship. 17. **conference:** conversation. [S.H.] 21. **enforced:** forced, constrained. 22. **tricks:** i.e., tricks of ceremony, ceremonious words and acts.—**plain:** open.—**simple:** without duplicity, guileless.

But hollow men, like horses hot at hand,
Make gallant show and promise of their mettle;

*Low march within.*

But when they should endure the bloody spur,                          25
They fall their crests, and like deceitful jades
Sink in the trial. Comes his army on?

LUCIL.     They mean this night in Sardis to be quarter'd.
The greater part, the horse in general,
Are come with Cassius.

BRU.                 Hark! He is arriv'd.                          30
March gently on to meet him.

*Enter* Cassius *and his* Powers.

CASS.     Stand, ho!

BRU.      Stand, ho! Speak the word along.

1. SOLD.   Stand!

2. SOLD.   Stand!                          35

3. SOLD.   Stand!

CASS.     Most noble brother, you have done me wrong.

BRU.      Judge me, you gods! wrong I mine enemies?
And if not so, how should I wrong a brother?

CASS.     Brutus, this sober form of yours hides wrongs;                          40
And when you do them—

BRU.                Cassius, be content.
Speak your griefs softly. I do know you well.
Before the eyes of both our armies here
(Which should perceive nothing but love from us)
Let us not wrangle. Bid them move away.                          45
Then in my tent, Cassius, enlarge your griefs,
And I will give you audience.

CASS.              Pindarus,
Bid our commanders lead their charges off
A little from this ground.

---

23. **hollow:** insincere.—**hot at hand:** full of spirit when held in, restless or impetuous when curbed. 24.
**mettle:** high spirit. 26. **fall:** let fall, droop.—**crests:** the crest is the upper part of the neck.—**jades:** a
contemptuous term for "horses." 27. **Sink:** give way, fail. 28. **Sardis:** the capital of Lydia in Asia Minor
(east of modern Izmir). [S.H.] 29. **horse in general:** the majority of the cavalry. [S.H.] 31. **gently:** slowly.
37. **brother:** see note on 2.1.70. 40. **this sober form:** this grave demeanour. 41. **be content:** calm yourself.
42. **griefs:** grievances. 46. **enlarge:** set at large, liberate; hence, as here, express freely. 48. **their charges:**
the troops they command.

Bru.     Lucilius, do you the like; and let no man                          50
         Come to our tent till we have done our conference.
         Let Lucius and Titinius guard our door.                   *Exeunt.*

Scene III. [*The camp near Sardis. Within the tent of* Brutus.]

*Enter* Brutus *and* Cassius.

Cass.    That you have wrong'd me doth appear in this:
         You have condemn'd and noted Lucius Pella
         For taking bribes here of the Sardians;
         Wherein my letters, praying on his side,
         Because I knew the man, were slighted off.                   5

Bru.     You wrong'd yourself to write in such a case.

Cass.    In such a time as this it is not meet
         That every nice offense should bear his comment.

Bru.     Let me tell you, Cassius, you yourself
         Are much condemn'd to have an itching palm,                 10
         To sell and mart your offices for gold
         To undeservers.

Cass.                     I an itching palm?
         You know that you are Brutus that speaks this,
         Or, by the gods, this speech were else your last!

Bru.     The name of Cassius honors this corruption,                 15
         And chastisement doth therefore hide his head.

Cass.    Chastisement?

Bru.     Remember March; the ides of March remember.
         Did not great Julius bleed for justice sake?
         What villain touch'd his body that did stab                 20
         And not for justice? What, shall one of us,

**Scene III.**

This scene is as vital an element in the tragedy as Antony's funeral oration. The dramatic purpose of the quarrel (which is quite historical) is to mark the foreordained downfall of the conspirators. Shakespeare has, as usual, treated times and places with freedom. In fact, the meeting of Brutus and Cassius at Sardis took place early in 42 B.C., and there were, according to Plutarch, two quarrels, which are here skillfully worked together. Philippi (in Macedonia) was hundreds of miles from Sardis (in Lydia)—considerably farther than Shakespeare seems to make it. 2. **noted:** marked with infamy, disgraced. 5. **slighted off:** put aside with scant attention. 8. **That...comment:** that every trivial fault should have its comment, should receive notice. 10. **condemn'd to have:** accused of having.—**an itching palm:** an old phrase for "a covetous disposition." Brutus does not accuse Cassius of taking bribes: he merely warns him of the necessity of avoiding such suspicion. 11. **mart:** traffic in. 16. **chastisement doth therefore hide his head:** people become reluctant to chide and criticize. [S.H.]

That struck the foremost man of all this world
But for supporting robbers—shall we now
Contaminate our fingers with base bribes,
And sell the mighty space of our large honors          25
For so much trash as may be grasped thus?
I had rather be a dog and bay the moon
Than such a Roman.

Cass.                          Brutus, bait not me!
I'll not endure it. You forget yourself
To hedge me in. I am a soldier, I,                     30
Older in practice, abler than yourself
To make conditions.

Bru.                          Go to! You are not, Cassius.

Cass.    I am.

Bru.    I say you are not.

Cass.    Urge me no more! I shall forget myself.        35
Have mind upon your health. Tempt me no farther.

Bru.    Away, slight man!

Cass.    Is't possible?

Bru.                          Hear me, for I will speak.
Must I give way and room to your rash choler?
Shall I be frighted when a madman stares?              40

Cass.    O ye gods, ye gods! Must I endure all this?

Bru.    All this? Ay, more! Fret till your proud heart break.
Go show your slaves how choleric you are
And make your bondmen tremble. Must I budge?
Must I observe you? Must I stand and crouch            45
Under your testy humor? By the gods,

---

23. **But for supporting robbers:** It has often been noticed that this was not the cause which prompted Brutus to attack Caesar. Extortion, however, is always an accompaniment of tyranny, so that this particular motive may well be regarded as involved in the general one. 26. **trash:** a common term of contempt for "money."—**thus:** in one's hand (with a gesture). 27. **bay the moon:** "to bark against the moon" is a proverbial phrase for ridiculous futility. 28. **bait not me:** do not harass me in this fashion. The figure is from bear-baiting (cf. 4.1.49). 30. **hedge me in:** limit my authority by your direction or censure. 32. **To make conditions:** to settle the terms in any negotiation—hence, in a more general sense, to manage affairs.—**Go to!** Here simply a term of expostulation. 35-36. **Urge...Tempt:** irritate...try. Both words mean practically the same thing as *bait* in line 28.—**health:** safety and welfare. 37. **slight man:** frivolous man, trifler. 39. **give...choler:** allow free course and scope to your quick temper. 43. **choleric:** prone to anger, irritable. 44. **bondmen:** slaves. [S.H.]—**budge:** flinch, wince. [S.H.] 45. **observe you:** show you reverence, be obsequious to you. 46. **testy humor:** irritability. [S.H.]

You shall digest the venom of your spleen,
Though it do split you; for from this day forth
I'll use you for my mirth, yea, for my laughter,
When you are waspish.

Cass.                              Is it come to this?                      50

Bru.    You say you are a better soldier.
Let it appear so; make your vaunting true,
And it shall please me well. For mine own part,
I shall be glad to learn of noble men.

Cass.   You wrong me every way! You wrong me, Brutus!      55
I said an elder soldier, not a better.
Did I say 'better'?

Bru.                   If you did, I care not.

Cass.   When Caesar liv'd he durst not thus have mov'd me.

Bru.    Peace, peace! You durst not so have tempted him.

Cass.   I durst not?                                                    60

Bru.    No.

Cass.   What, durst not tempt him?

Bru.                              For your life you durst not.

Cass.   Do not presume too much upon my love.
I may do that I shall be sorry for.

Bru.    You have done that you should be sorry for.          65
There is no terror, Cassius, in your threats;
For I am arm'd so strong in honesty
That they pass by me as the idle wind,
Which I respect not. I did send to you
For certain sums of gold, which you denied me;          70
For I can raise no money by vile means.
By heaven, I had rather coin my heart

---

47-48. **You shall digest...you:** The spleen was supposed to be the seat of various sudden fits of emotion, such as uncontrollable laughter, irascibility, nervousness, and the like. The exact meaning of the passage is: "When the action of your spleen produces irritation in your mind, you shall not relieve yourself by expressing it, but you shall keep it to yourself, digesting or assimilating it as best you can." 50. **waspish:** irritable. [S.H.] 52. **vaunting:** boasting. [S.H.] 54. **noble men:** Brutus means that it will afford him pleasure to hear of the existence of good soldiers and noble men; he implies that, up to the present moment, Cassius has given no evidence of being either. 57. **If you did, I care not:** this does not mean "I don't care what you said" in the irritatingly indifferent sense of the modern phrase, but rather, "Whatever your insult was to me, I can bear it with equanimity, for I regard neither your boasts nor your anger." 59. **tempted:** tried, tested, provoked. 63. **Do not presume too much upon:** do not count too much on. [S.H.] 67. **honesty:** rectitude, consciousness of my own virtue. 69-70. **respect not:** heed not, pay no attention to.—**I did send...denied me:** this is the grievance at which Brutus had hinted in 4.2.

|  | And drop my blood for drachmas than to wring |  |
|  | From the hard hands of peasants their vile trash |  |
|  | By any indirection. I did send | 75 |
|  | To you for gold to pay my legions, |  |
|  | Which you denied me. Was that done like Cassius? |  |
|  | Should I have answer'd Caius Cassius so? |  |
|  | When Marcus Brutus grows so covetous |  |
|  | To lock such rascal counters from his friends, | 80 |
|  | Be ready, gods, with all your thunderbolts, |  |
|  | Dash him to pieces! |  |

CASS.                        I denied you not.

BRU.        You did.

CASS.        I did not. He was but a fool that brought
My answer back. Brutus hath riv'd my heart.                    85
A friend should bear his friend's infirmities,
But Brutus makes mine greater than they are.

BRU.        I do not, till you practice them on me.

CASS.        You love me not.

BRU.                        I do not like your faults.

CASS.        A friendly eye could never see such faults.                    90

BRU.        A flatterer's would not, though they do appear
As huge as high Olympus.

CASS.        Come, Antony, and young Octavius, come!
Revenge yourselves alone on Cassius.
For Cassius is aweary of the world:                    95
Hated by one he loves; brav'd by his brother;
Check'd like a bondman; all his faults observ'd,
Set in a notebook, learn'd and conn'd by rote
To cast into my teeth. O, I could weep
My spirit from mine eyes! There is my dagger,                    100

---

73. **drop:** spill. [S.H.] 74. **trash:** cf. 4.3.26. 75. **indirection:** unjust or illegal means. Brutus does not accuse Cassius of extortion: he says merely that he himself had been in such straits for money that he could raise it only by such means—and this, he declares, he was unwilling to do; therefore he had sent to Cassius for help, knowing that he was well supplied. 80. **To lock:** as to lock, as to deny. [S.H.]—**such rascal counters:** such wretched coins. Counters were properly pieces of uncurrent coin employed by shopkeepers and others to assist in "counting" or making computations; hence the word is often used as a contemptuous term for "money." A *rascal,* in Shakespeare's time, meant usually "one of the rabble," "a low fellow." Hence, as an adjective, the word is a synonym for *vile* (74). 84. **He was but a fool:** the messenger who brought you my answer to your request for money did not understand my message. 85. **riv'd:** split. [S.H.] 86. **infirmities:** shortcomings. [S.H.] 92. **Olympus:** see note 3.1.74. [S.H.] 96. **brav'd:** defied. [S.H.] 97. **Check'd:** rebuked, chided. 98. **conn'd by rote:** memorized, learned by heart. [S.H.] 99. **cast into my teeth:** throw in my face. [S.H.]

And here my naked breast; within, a heart
Dearer than Pluto's mine, richer than gold.
If that thou be'st a Roman, take it forth.
I, that denied thee gold, will give my heart.
Strike as thou didst at Caesar; for I know,                    105
When thou didst hate him worst, thou lov'dst him better
Than ever thou lov'dst Cassius.

BRU.                                    Sheathe your dagger.
Be angry when you will; it shall have scope.
Do what you will; dishonor shall be humor.
O Cassius, you are yoked with a lamb                            110
That carries anger as the flint bears fire;
Who, much enforced, shows a hasty spark,
And straight is cold again.

CASS.                              Hath Cassius liv'd
To be but mirth and laughter to his Brutus
When grief and blood ill-temper'd vexeth him?                   115

BRU. When I spoke that, I was ill-temper'd too.

CASS. Do you confess so much? Give me your hand.

BRU. And my heart too.

CASS.                          O Brutus!

BRU.                                What's the matter?

CASS. Have not you love enough to bear with me
When that rash humor which my mother gave me                    120
Makes me forgetful?

BRU.                        Yes, Cassius; and from henceforth,
When you are over-earnest with your Brutus,
He'll think your mother chides, and leave you so.

*Enter a* Poet [*followed by* Lucilius, Titinius, *and* Lucius].

---

102. **Dearer:** more precious.—**Pluto's mine:** Pluto was the god of the underworld and, as such, lord of mines of gold and silver. 104. **I, that denied thee gold:** I, that, *as thou dost allege,* refused thee gold. Cassius does not here take back his assertion made in line 82: "I denied you not." On the contrary, he argues passionately that his willingness to "give his heart" is proof that he did not really refuse the lesser gift of money. And Brutus believes him, as the next speech shows. 108. **scope:** free play. 109. **dishonor shall be humor:** any insults you offer me, I will excuse as merely an effect of your irritable disposition. 110. **a lamb:** Brutus is characterizing himself. 112. **much enforced:** subjected to great provocation. 113. **straight:** straightway. 115. **blood ill-temper'd:** an ill-compounded disposition. 120. **that rash humor:** that hasty or irritable temperament. Cassius's remark that this was inherited from his mother is Shakespeare's own invention—a vivid detail, like Caesar's deafness in 1.2.213. 123. **your mother chides:** i.e., it is merely your inherited disposition that makes you speak irritably.—**leave you so:** let it go at that.

| | |
|---|---|
| POET. | Let me go in to see the generals! |
| | There is some grudge between 'em. 'Tis not meet    125 |
| | They be alone. |
| LUCIL. | You shall not come to them. |
| POET. | Nothing but death shall stay me. |
| CASS. | How now? What's the matter? |
| POET. | For shame, you generals! What do you mean?    130 |
| | Love and be friends, as two such men should be; |
| | For I have seen more years, I'm sure, than ye. |
| CASS. | Ha, ha! How vilely doth this cynic rhyme! |
| BRU. | Get you hence, sirrah! Saucy fellow, hence! |
| CASS. | Bear with him, Brutus. 'Tis his fashion.    135 |
| BRU. | I'll know his humor when he knows his time. |
| | What should the wars do with these jigging fools? |
| | Companion, hence! |
| CASS. | Away, away, be gone!    *Exit* Poet. |
| BRU. | Lucilius and Titinius, bid the commanders |
| | Prepare to lodge their companies tonight.    140 |
| CASS. | And come yourselves, and bring Messala with you |
| | Immediately to us.    [*Exeunt* Lucilius *and* Titinius.] |
| BRU. | Lucius, a bowl of wine.    [*Exit* Lucius.] |
| CASS. | I did not think you could have been so angry. |
| BRU. | O Cassius, I am sick of many griefs. |
| CASS. | Of your philosophy you make no use    145 |
| | If you give place to accidental evils. |
| BRU. | No man bears sorrow better. Portia is dead. |
| CASS. | Ha! Portia? |

124. The episode that follows is the dramatization of a ludicrous incident in North's Plutarch. The intruder, one Marcus Phaonius, was not a poet, but a kind of Cynic philosopher. He quoted poetry, however, to the generals, and Shakespeare simplifies matters by giving him credit for the verses. 125. **grudge:** ill feeling. 131. **Love and be friends:** this doggerel amuses Cassius; but Brutus, who has no sense of humor and a strong feeling of personal dignity, is offended at the intrusive rhymester. 133. **cynic:** rude man. [S.H.] 134. **sirrah:** often used in angry or contemptuous address. Cf. 3.1.10, and note. 136. **I'll know...time:** I will admit his right to be eccentric when he chooses a proper occasion to exhibit his eccentricity. 137. **jigging:** rhyming. A contemptuous word. A *jig* was, in one of its meanings, a comic song or a comic dialog in verse. 138. **Companion:** fellow. Common in this contemptuous sense. 145-146. **Of your philosophy...evils:** Brutus was a Stoic and as such his belief was that nothing evil could happen to a good man. In other words, he held that what Cassius calls "accidental evils" (i.e., "misfortunes that come from the chances of life") should be and are indifferent to the philosopher.—**give place:** give way, yield.

BRU.    She is dead.

CASS.   How scap'd I killing when I cross'd you so?            150
O insupportable and touching loss!
Upon what sickness?

BRU.                    Impatient of my absence,
And grief that young Octavius with Mark Antony
Have made themselves so strong; for with her death
That tidings came. With this she fell distract,            155
And (her attendants absent) swallow'd fire.

CASS.   And died so?

BRU.                    Even so.

CASS.                    O ye immortal gods!

*Enter* Boy [Lucius], *with wine and tapers.*

BRU.    Speak no more of her. Give me a bowl of wine.
In this I bury all unkindness, Cassius.            *Drinks.*

CASS.   My heart is thirsty for that noble pledge.            160
Fill, Lucius, till the wine o'erswell the cup.
I cannot drink too much of Brutus' love.    [*Drinks. Exit Lucius.*]

*Enter* Titinius *and* Messala.

BRU.    Come in, Titinius! Welcome, good Messala.
Now sit we close about this taper here
And call in question our necessities.            165

CASS.   Portia, art thou gone?

BRU.                    No more, I pray you.
Messala, I have here received letters
That young Octavius and Mark Antony
Come down upon us with a mighty power,
Bending their expedition toward Philippi.            170

MES.    Myself have letters of the selfsame tenure.

BRU.    With what addition?

MES.    That by proscription and bills of outlawry

---

152-153. **Upon:** in consequence of. 156. **swallow'd fire:** This common but improbable story with regard to Portia is found in Plutarch and other ancient writers. 165. **call in question:** discuss. *Question* often means simply "conversation." 169. **power:** force, troop, army. 170. **Bending their expedition:** directing their march with speed. 171. **tenure:** tenor, meaning. 173. **bills of outlawry:** proscription lists. Citizens who were proscribed were put outside the protection of the law: it was not only legal to kill them, but rewards were offered for their death.

|  | Octavius, Antony, and Lepidus |  |
|  | Have put to death an hundred senators. | 175 |
| Bru. | Therein our letters do not well agree. |  |
|  | Mine speak of seventy senators that died |  |
|  | By their proscriptions, Cicero being one. |  |
| Cass. | Cicero one? |  |
| Mes. | Cicero is dead, |  |
|  | And by that order of proscription. | 180 |
|  | Had you your letters from your wife, my lord? |  |
| Bru. | No, Messala. |  |
| Mes. | Nor nothing in your letters writ of her? |  |
| Bru. | Nothing, Messala. |  |
| Mes. | That methinks is strange. |  |
| Bru. | Why ask you? Hear you aught of her in yours? | 185 |
| Mes. | No, my lord. |  |
| Bru. | Now as you are a Roman, tell me true. |  |
| Mes. | Then like a Roman bear the truth I tell; |  |
|  | For certain she is dead, and by strange manner. |  |
| Bru. | Why, farewell, Portia. We must die, Messala. | 190 |
|  | With meditating that she must die once, |  |
|  | I have the patience to endure it now. |  |
| Mes. | Even so great men great losses should endure. |  |
| Cass. | I have as much of this in art as you, |  |
|  | But yet my nature could not bear it so. | 195 |
| Bru. | Well, to our work alive. What do you think |  |
|  | Of marching to Philippi presently? |  |
| Cass. | I do not think it good. |  |

---

178. **Cicero being one:** Cicero was put on the proscription list through the base ingratitude of Octavius, whose cause he had warmly espoused against Antony. These facts, however, are not brought out by Shakespeare, who makes Antony and Octavius friendly from the outset (3.1.276-297; 3.2.267-276) and represents them as instantly joining forces to avenge Caesar. 183. **writ of her:** have been written about her. [S.H.] 184 ff. **Nothing, Messala:** what follows in 181–195 flatly contradicts Brutus's own words to Cassius just before (147-156). It is possible that Shakespeare intended to omit this second announcement. However, the two moments can make sense in performance, as Brutus can first show emotional vulnerability and then the fortitude expected of a philosopher. [S.H.] 185. **aught:** anything. [S.H.] 192. **patience:** fortitude. 194. **in art:** in theory. "I fully understand the tenets of the Stoic philosophy with regard to fortitude, but I could not control my natural emotions as you do." 196. **to our work alive:** Let us go about the work which we, as living men, have to do. 197. **presently:** immediately.

| | |
|---|---|
| BRU. | Your reason? |
| CASS. | This it is: |

'Tis better that the enemy seek us.
So shall he waste his means, weary his soldiers,                                      200
Doing himself offense, whilst we, lying still,
Are full of rest, defense, and nimbleness.

BRU.    Good reasons must of force give place to better.
The people 'twixt Philippi and this ground
Do stand but in a forc'd affection;                                                          205
For they have grudg'd us contribution.
The enemy, marching along by them,
By them shall make a fuller number up,
Come on refresh'd, new-added, and encourag'd;
From which advantage shall we cut him off                                          210
If at Philippi we do face him there,
These people at our back.

CASS.                                          Hear me, good brother.

BRU.    Under your pardon. You must note beside
That we have tried the utmost of our friends,
Our legions are brimful, our cause is ripe.                                            215
The enemy increaseth every day;
We, at the height, are ready to decline.
There is a tide in the affairs of men
Which, taken at the flood, leads on to fortune;
Omitted, all the voyage of their life                                                       220
Is bound in shallows and in miseries.
On such a full sea are we now afloat,
And we must take the current when it serves
Or lose our ventures.

CASS.                                          Then, with your will, go on.
We'll along ourselves and meet them at Philippi.                                225

---

201. **offense:** harm. 203. **Good reasons...better:** Brutus here, as always, insists on having his own way and imposes his stronger will upon the judgment of Cassius. It is a part of the tragedy that in such cases Brutus's judgment is usually wrong and that of the less noble and more selfish Cassius right.—**of force:** perforce, of necessity. 205. **Do stand but in a forc'd affection:** are favorable to us, not heartily, but merely by compulsion. 209. **new-added:** reinforced. 213. **Under your pardon:** the solemn obstinacy of Brutus comes out with great effect in this scene. That it should determine the fate of the conspirators is an example of what is regularly called tragic irony. 220. **Omitted:** neglected, let slip. 221. **bound:** bounded, confined.—**in shallows and in miseries:** An example of common rhetorical usage by which a figurative word is immediately explained by a literal synonym, the two being connected by *and*. 224. **our ventures:** a figure from seafaring. The amount invested in a ship or cargo was regularly spoken of as a man's *venture*; and persons who took risks of this kind were called *adventurers*. 224. **with your will:** in accordance with your wish.

BRU.        The deep of night is crept upon our talk
           And nature must obey necessity,
           Which we will niggard with a little rest.
           There is no more to say?

CASS.                     No more. Good night.
           Early tomorrow will we rise and hence.                    230

BRU.        Lucius! [*Enter* Lucius.] My gown. [*Exit* Lucius.] Farewell, good
               Messala.
           Good night, Titinius. Noble, noble Cassius,
           Good night and good repose!

CASS.                          O my dear brother,
           This was an ill beginning of the night!
           Never come such division 'tween our souls!                235
           Let it not, Brutus.

                    *Enter* Lucius, *with the gown.*

BRU.                   Everything is well.

CASS.       Good night, my lord.

BRU.                     Good night, good brother.

TIT., MES.  Good night, Lord Brutus.

BRU.                       Farewell every one.

                    *Exeunt* [Cassius, Titinius, *and* Messala].
           Give me the gown. Where is thy instrument?

LUC.        Here in the tent.

BRU.                      What, thou speak'st drowsily?              240
           Poor knave, I blame thee not; thou art o'er-watch'd.
           Call Claudius and some other of my men;
           I'll have them sleep on cushions in my tent.

LUC.        Varro and Claudius!

                    *Enter* Varro *and* Claudius.

VAR.        Calls my lord?                                           245

---

228. **Which we will niggard with a little rest:** nature yields to necessity, and we must sleep; but we will scant nature by making our sleep short. 241. **knave:** the original meaning of *knave* is "boy." Like *boy,* it is often used for "servant."—**o'er-watch'd:** worn out by late hours. *To watch* often means, not "to exercise vigilance," but simply "to keep awake."

BRU.    I pray you, sirs, lie in my tent and sleep.
        It may be I shall raise you by-and-by
        On business to my brother Cassius.

VAR.    So please you, we will stand and watch your pleasure.

BRU.    I will not have it so. Lie down, good sirs.                          250
        It may be I shall otherwise bethink me.
                                [Varro *and* Claudius *lie down.*]
        Look, Lucius, here's the book I sought for so;
        I put it in the pocket of my gown.

LUC.    I was sure your lordship did not give it me.

BRU.    Bear with me, good boy, I am much forgetful.                        255
        Canst thou hold up thy heavy eyes awhile,
        And touch thy instrument a strain or two?

LUC.    Ay, my lord, an't please you.

BRU.                                It does, my boy.
        I trouble thee too much, but thou art willing.

LUC.    It is my duty, sir.                                                 260

BRU.    I should not urge thy duty past thy might.
        I know young bloods look for a time of rest.

LUC.    I have slept, my lord, already.

BRU.    It was well done; and thou shalt sleep again;
        I will not hold thee long. If I do live,                           265
        I will be good to thee.    *Music, and a song.* [Lucius *falls asleep.*]
        This is a sleepy tune. O murd'rous slumber!
        Layest thou thy leaden mace upon my boy,
        That plays thee music? Gentle knave, good night.
        I will not do thee so much wrong to wake thee.                     270
        If thou dost nod, thou break'st thy instrument;
        I'll take it from thee; and, good boy, good night.
        Let me see, let me see. Is not the leaf turn'd down
        Where I left reading? Here it is, I think.                  [*Sits.*]

---

247. **raise:** call up, rouse. 248. **my brother Cassius:** see note on 2.1.70. 249. **watch your pleasure:** be on the watch for any wish you may have. 250. **I will not have it so:** the amiability and humanity of Brutus toward his servants and subordinates is no less striking than his dignified self-will with his equals. 251. **I shall otherwise bethink me:** I shall change my mind. [S.H.] 258. **an't:** if it. [S.H.] 261. **might:** physical strength. 262. **young bloods:** youthful constitutions. 267. **murderous slumber:** deep sleep (which resembles death). [S.H.] 268. **mace:** the staff carried by a sheriff's officer with which he touches on the shoulder the person he arrests. 270. **to wake thee:** as to wake thee.

Caesar's ghost in the 1979 BBC version (4.3.275).

*Enter the* Ghost of Caesar.†

How ill this taper burns! Ha! who comes here?                                  275
I think it is the weakness of mine eyes
That shapes this monstrous apparition.
It comes upon me. Art thou anything?
Art thou some god, some angel, or some devil,
That mak'st my blood cold and my hair to stare?                                280
Speak to me what thou art.

GHOST        Thy evil spirit, Brutus.

---

275. **How ill this taper burns!** It was a common belief that lights grow dim when a ghost or evil spirit is near. 277. **monstrous:** portentous. 278. **upon:** against. 279. **Art thou some god,** etc. This does not show that Brutus fails to recognize the likeness of the apparition to Caesar (a likeness which would at once be clear to the audience), but merely that he is in doubt as to its character. It was a common belief that spirits who were not ghosts might appear to one in the form of some departed friend or enemy. That Brutus finally decided that he had seen Caesar's ghost is clear from his words to Volumnius in 5.5.17–19. This is indeed "Caesar's spirit, ranging for revenge" (3.1.270). 280. **to stare:** to stand on end.

---

†     In Bradley's film, the Ghost of Caesar appears as a face within the flame of a taper. The face is lit in a way that makes it appear as a skull, emphasizing its deadly and supernatural aspect. In Burge's production, the Ghost also appears within the flame of a candle, but this time his whole body can be seen, wearing the blood-covered toga in which he was killed. Once again, Burge emphasizes the gory aspects of the assassination. In the BBC version, the Ghost's face invades the whole right side of the screen, reproducing Caesar's omnipresence even after his death. Mankiewicz's film insists even more on this spirit of Caesar that can never be eradicated. The Ghost appears as an eerie, ethereal figure, flickering in the curtains of Brutus's tent. Brutus takes his sword and rushes toward the apparition, attempting to reproduce the stabbing gesture he had accomplished during the murder. But the Ghost suddenly disappears, leaving Brutus both frustrated and afraid: Caesar's spirit cannot be killed as his body was. [S.H.]

Caesar's ghost in Bradley's 1950 film (4.3.275).

| | | |
|---|---|---|
| BRU. | Why com'st thou? | |
| GHOST | To tell thee thou shalt see me at Philippi. | |
| BRU. | Well; then I shall see thee again? | |
| GHOST | Ay, at Philippi. | 285 |
| BRU. | Why, I will see thee at Philippi then.     [*Exit* Ghost.] | |
| | Now I have taken heart thou vanishest. | |
| | Ill spirit, I would hold more talk with thee. | |
| | Boy! Lucius! Varro! Claudius! Sirs! Awake! Claudius! | |
| LUC. | The strings, my lord, are false. | 290 |
| BRU. | He thinks he still is at his instrument. | |
| | Lucius, awake! | |
| LUC. | My lord? | |
| BRU. | Didst thou dream, Lucius, that thou so criedst out? | |
| LUC. | My lord, I do not know that I did cry. | 295 |
| BRU. | Yes, that thou didst. Didst thou see anything? | |
| LUC. | Nothing, my lord. | |
| BRU. | Sleep again, Lucius. Sirrah Claudius! | |
| | [*To* Varro] Fellow thou, awake! | |

290. **false:** out of tune.

| VAR.  | My lord? | 300 |
| CLAU. | My lord? | |
| BRU.  | Why did you so cry out, sirs, in your sleep? | |
| BOTH  | Did we, my lord? | |
| BRU.  | Ay. Saw you anything? | |
| VAR.  | No, my lord, I saw nothing. | |
| CLAU. | Nor I, my lord. | |
| BRU.  | Go and commend me to my brother Cassius. | 305 |
|       | Bid him set on his pow'rs betimes before, | |
|       | And we will follow. | |
| BOTH  | It shall be done, my lord.        *Exeunt.* | |

# ACT V

## SCENE I. [*Near Philippi.*]

*Enter* Octavius, Antony, *and their* Army.†

OCT.    Now, Antony, our hopes are answered.
        You said the enemy would not come down
        But keep the hills and upper regions.

---

305. **commend me:** give my greetings. 306. **set on his pow'rs:** advance his forces—**betimes:** early in the morning. [S.H.]

ACT V. SCENE I.

Between Act IV and Act V time enough has elapsed to enable the army of Brutus and Cassius to march from Sardis in Lydia to Philippi in Macedonia. The meeting at Sardis occurred, in historical fact, early in 42 B.C. and the Battle of Philippi took place in the following autumn. 1. **answered:** met, fulfilled.

---

†    The battle sequence in Mankiewicz's 1953 film recycles the codes of the Western genre. To the beating of Native American drums, Cassius and Brutus's soldiers march in a narrow, barren pass, reminiscient of a Wild West canyon. Above them, Mark Antony, smiling mischievously, orders his army to launch arrows and spears. Antony and his army are in the same position as Indians attacking the US cavalry in a classic western. Mankiewicz thus blurs the notion of good and evil in his film—Antony is not a spotless hero, nor Brutus a heroic victim. Burge's 1970 epic film displays impressive human means to produce a very realistic, full-blown battle. While some grand martial music is played, the camera slowly pans across a mountainous landscape to reveal several marching legions. This long take ends when the camera finally finds the face of a powerful Octavius, watching his troops with ease and pleasure. In this shot, Octavius takes over the whole scenery and the army, anticipating his future status as emperor. The following discussion between Antony and Octavious is extremely relaxed. Antony is eating fruit, lying at ease on the ground. The scene explicitly foresees their easy victory. [S.H.]

|  | It proves not so. Their battles are at hand; |  |
|--|--|--|
|  | They mean to warn us at Philippi here, | 5 |
|  | Answering before we do demand of them. |  |
| Ant. | Tut! I am in their bosoms and I know |  |
|  | Wherefore they do it. They could be content |  |
|  | To visit other places, and come down |  |
|  | With fearful bravery, thinking by this face | 10 |
|  | To fasten in our thoughts that they have courage. |  |
|  | But 'tis not so. |  |

*Enter a* Messenger.

|  |  |  |
|--|--|--|
| Mess. | Prepare you, generals. |  |
|  | The enemy comes on in gallant show; |  |
|  | Their bloody sign of battle is hung out, |  |
|  | And something to be done immediately. | 15 |
| Ant. | Octavius, lead your battle softly on |  |
|  | Upon the left hand of the even field. |  |
| Oct. | Upon the right hand I. Keep thou the left. |  |
| Ant. | Why do you cross me in this exigent? |  |
| Oct. | I do not cross you; but I will do so. | *March.* 20 |

*Drum. Enter* Brutus, Cassius, *and their* Army;
[Lucilius, Titinius, Messala, *and others*].

|  |  |  |
|--|--|--|
| Bru. | They stand and would have parley. |  |
| Cass. | Stand fast, Titinius. We must out and talk. |  |
| Oct. | Mark Antony, shall we give sign of battle? |  |
| Ant. | No, Caesar, we will answer on their charge. |  |

---

4. **battles:** armies. 5. **to warn us:** to summon us, to challenge us to fight. 6. **Answering:** appearing in opposition to us.—**demand of them:** call them to battle; literally, ask [it] of them. 7. **I am in their bosoms:** I understand their secret thoughts. 8. **Wherefore:** why. [S.H.]—**could be content:** would like, would prefer. 10. **With fearful bravery:** in magnificent array, but with timorous hearts. *Fearful* may, of course, mean "terrible," but note the context. *Bravery* also suggests "defiance." It never means merely "courage" in Shakespeare.—**face:** appearance, outward show. 11. **fasten in our thoughts:** convince us. [S.H.] 14. **Their bloody sign of battle:** the red flag (*vexillum*) which, when hung out at the general's tent, signified immediate attack. 16. **softly:** slowly. 18. **Upon the right hand I:** cf. North's Plutarch: "*Brutus* praied *Cassius* he might haue the leading of the right wing, the which men thought was farre meeter for *Cassius:* both because he was the elder man, and also for that he had the better experience. But yet *Cassius* gaue it him." Shakespeare shifts the incident to the other army. 19. **in this exigent:** in this exigency, at this critical moment. 20. **I do not cross you...do so:** I am not opposing your wishes out of mere perversity—I simply express my own determination. *Will* is dispassionately emphatic (cf. 2.2.71: "The cause is in my will"). In this brief speech, Octavius asserts himself as the superior of Antony in moral and intellectual force. 21. **parley:** conference. [S.H.] 24. **we will answer on their charge:** we will meet their attack when they make it.

|        | Make forth. The generals would have some words. | 25 |
|--------|--------------------------------------------------|----|
| Oct.   | Stir not until the signal.                       |    |
| Bru.   | Words before blows. Is it so, countrymen?        |    |
| Oct.   | Not that we love words better, as you do.        |    |
| Bru.   | Good words are better than bad strokes, Octavius. |   |

Ant.  In your bad strokes, Brutus, you give good words;      30
Witness the hole you made in Caesar's heart,
Crying 'Long live! Hail, Caesar!'

Cass.                                         Antony,
The posture of your blows are yet unknown;
But for your words, they rob the Hybla bees,
And leave them honeyless.

Ant.                                  Not stingless too.      35

Bru.  O yes, and soundless too!
For you have stol'n their buzzing, Antony,
And very wisely threat before you sting.

Ant.  Villains! you did not so when your vile daggers
Hack'd one another in the sides of Caesar.                  40
You show'd your teeth like apes, and fawn'd like hounds,
And bow'd like bondmen, kissing Caesar's feet;
Whilst damned Casca, like a cur, behind
Struck Caesar on the neck. O you flatterers!

Cass.  Flatterers? Now, Brutus, thank yourself!              45
This tongue had not offended so today
If Cassius might have rul'd.

Oct.  Come, come, the cause! If arguing make us sweat,
The proof of it will turn to redder drops.

---

25. **Make forth:** step forward. 27 ff. What follows is a curious example of a very old custom. In Shakespeare, it appears almost like a literary survival of what is constantly found in older Germanic literature. Before two hosts met in battle, the leaders were expected, in the heroic age, to exchange taunts. Such a conversation is technically known as a *flyting.* 33. **The posture of your blows are:** the kind of blows that you will give. The plural verb is due to the intervention of the plural noun *blows.* 34. **for:** as for.—**Hybla:** a mountain (and a town) in Sicily, famous for honey. The honeyed words of Antony are his professions of friendship for the conspirators immediately after the assassination of Caesar (3.1.184-190, 220-222). 35. **Not stingless too:** Antony tauntingly suggests that his words must leave a sting in the conspirator's hearts. 39. **you did not so:** you did not threaten or give warning before you struck. 41. **like apes:** in smiles like an ape's grin, which one cannot trust, since he may mean to bite. Performing apes were common in Shakespeare's time and are often mentioned in the drama. 47. **might have rul'd:** could have had his way. Cassius had advised the death of Antony, but Brutus had opposed it, refusing to believe that he could prove dangerous (2.1.155 ff.). 48. **the cause!** Let us come to the point! The cold-blooded and clear-headed Octavius is impatient at this idle wrangling. He states "the cause" briefly in the next lines: "Punishment for the traitors!" 49. **The proof of it:** the testing of the argument by an actual struggle.

Look,                                                             50
I draw a sword against conspirators.
When think you that the sword goes up again?
Never, till Caesar's three-and-thirty wounds
Be well aveng'd, or till another Caesar
Have added slaughter to the sword of traitors.                   55

BRU.    Caesar, thou canst not die by traitors' hands
Unless thou bring'st them with thee.

OCT.                                  So I hope.
I was not born to die on Brutus' sword.

BRU.    O, if thou wert the noblest of thy strain,
Young man, thou couldst not die more honorable.                  60

CASS.   A peevish schoolboy, worthless of such honor,
Join'd with a masker and a reveller!

ANT.    Old Cassius still.

OCT.                                  Come, Antony. Away!
Defiance, traitors, hurl we in your teeth.
If you dare fight today, come to the field;                      65
If not, when you have stomachs.

                         *Exeunt* Octavius, Antony, *and* Army.

CASS.   Why, now blow wind, swell billow, and swim bark!
The storm is up, and all is on the hazard.

BRU.    Ho, Lucilius! Hark, a word with you.        Lucilius *stands forth.*

LUCIL.                               My lord?

                    [Brutus *and* Lucilius *converse apart.*]

CASS.   Messala.                                    Messala *stands forth.*

MES.                    What says my general?

---

52. **up:** often used for "in (or into) the sheath." 53. **three-and-thirty:** probably a misprint for *three-and-twenty,* the number given by Plutarch, Appian, and Suetonius. Such mistakes in copying and in printing were very common on account of the practice of using Roman numerals. 54-55. **till another Caesar... traitors:** till I too, another Caesar, have by my death at your hands stained your traitorous swords with further slaughter. 56-57. **thou canst not...with thee:** a dignified way of disavowing the title of "traitor" and casting it back at Octavius and Antony. 59. **strain:** lineage, family. 60. **thou couldst not...honorable:** thou couldst not be more honored, meet with greater honor, in thy death. 61. **peevish:** childish, silly. Rather more common in this sense than in that of "fretful," "whining."—**worthless:** utterly unworthy. 62. **a masker and a reveller:** Antony's dissipation was notorious. A *masker* is, literally, one fond of engaging in the half-dramatic social entertainment known as the *masque,* which was, in its beginning, a masquerade on a small scale, but which ultimately developed into a form of dramatic art. 66. **stomachs:** appetites (for battle). 67. **swim bark:** let the ship sail. [S.H.] 68. **on the hazard:** a matter of chance. [S.H.]

CASS.                                  Messala,                          70
          This is my birthday; as this very day
          Was Cassius born. Give me thy hand, Messala.
          Be thou my witness that against my will
          (As Pompey was) am I compell'd to set
          Upon one battle all our liberties.                             75
          You know that I held Epicurus strong
          And his opinion. Now I change my mind
          And partly credit things that do presage.
          Coming from Sardis, on our former ensign
          Two mighty eagles fell; and there they perch'd,                80
          Gorging and feeding from our soldiers' hands,
          Who to Philippi here consorted us.
          This morning are they fled away and gone,
          And in their steads do ravens, crows, and kites
          Fly o'er our heads and downward look on us                     85
          As we were sickly prey.† Their shadows seem
          A canopy most fatal, under which
          Our army lies, ready to give up the ghost.

MES.      Believe not so.

CASS.                         I but believe it partly;
          For I am fresh of spirit and resolv'd                          90
          To meet all perils very constantly.

BRU.      Even so, Lucilius.

CASS.                           Now, most noble Brutus,
          The gods today stand friendly, that we may,

---

71. **as this very day:** i.e., simply "this very day." *As* was often prefixed to expressions of time without altering their meaning. 74. **As Pompey was:** before the Battle of Pharsalus Pompey had in his camp many impatient (but inexperienced) Roman nobles, who were clamorous for combat, while he himself wanted to avoid battle with Caesar. [S.H.]—**set:** stake, hazard. 76. **I held Epicurus strong:** I regarded Epicurus as right in his views. Cassius refers to the Epicurean belief that the gods do not trouble themselves about human affairs, and that therefore to regard the signs and omens by which the gods are thought to signify the future to men, is a ridiculous superstition. As a matter of history, Cassius did profess the Epicurean philosophy. 79. **former:** forward, foremost. 80. **fell:** swooped down. 82. **consorted:** accompanied. [S.H.] 84. **ravens, crows and kites:** birds of ill omen. [S.H.] 86. **As:** as if.—**sickly prey:** a condensed expression for "sick and likely to die and so to become their prey." 88. **give up the ghost:** die. [S.H.] 91. **constantly:** resolutely 92. **Even so, Lucilius:** this marks the end of the conversation between Lucilius and Brutus which began in l. 69. 93. **stand:** subjunctive expressing a wish: "May the gods today stand friendly." [S.H.]

---

†    In Burge's film, these lines by Cassius are illustrated by a shot of the sky in which crows are flying
     ominously. This shot creates a visual link with the start of the movie that showed birds of prey
     hovering above the battlefield strewn with corpses, where Pompey's son was defeated and where
     thousands of Romans lost their lives. The film thus insists upon a fateful and cyclical return of
     historical events and civil wars. [S.H.]

Lovers in peace, lead on our days to age! \
But since the affairs of men rest still incertain, 95 \
Let's reason with the worst that may befall. \
If we do lose this battle, then is this \
The very last time we shall speak together. \
What are you then determined to do?

BRU. Even by the rule of that philosophy 100 \
By which I did blame Cato for the death \
Which he did give himself—I know not how, \
But I do find it cowardly and vile, \
For fear of what might fall, so to prevent \
The time of life—arming myself with patience 105 \
To stay the providence of some high powers \
That govern us below.

CASS.              Then, if we lose this battle, \
You are contented to be led in triumph \
Thorough the streets of Rome.

BRU. No, Cassius, no. Think not, thou noble Roman, 110 \
That ever Brutus will go bound to Rome. \
He bears too great a mind. But this same day \
Must end that work the ides of March begun, \
And whether we shall meet again I know not. \
Therefore our everlasting farewell take. 115 \
For ever and for ever farewell, Cassius! \
If we do meet again, why, we shall smile; \
If not, why then this parting was well made.

---

94. **Lovers:** devoted friends. 95. **rest:** remain.—**still:** always. 96. **reason:** reckon. 100–107. **Even by the rule…below:** I mean to act according to the rule of that Stoic philosophy which made me blame Cato for his suicide (somehow, I find suicide cowardly)—that is, putting on the armor of fortitude, I mean to await whatever the powers above have appointed. The passage "I know not how…time of life" forms a parenthesis. The Stoics held that suicide is cowardly and wrong. A man in this life, they argued, is like a soldier at his post: to commit suicide is to desert. 101. **Cato:** Cato the younger, called Cato *Uticensis* ("of Utica") from the place of his death. He killed himself (46 B.C.) to avoid falling into the hands of Caesar, against whom he had held out on the Pompeian side until the last. The Roman Republicans—Caesar's opponents—had exalted Cato as the martyr of their cause. Brutus, his son-in-law, was sometimes regarded as his political successor. Plutarch records Brutus's change of mind about suicide. 102–105. **I know not how…time of life:** somehow or other I find it cowardly and unworthy of a man, for fear of what may happen to him in this world, thus to anticipate [by suicide] the term or natural limit of his life.—**prevent:** See 2.1.28, note. 105–107. **arming myself…below:** this forms the real answer to the question of Cassius in line 99: "What are you then determined to do?"—**stay:** await. The indefinite *some* is expressive: Brutus rejects the crudely imagined deities of the Roman religion, but he believes in "*some* high powers," whose exact nature he cannot define. 110. Brutus has just told Cassius that he is determined not to follow Cato's example in case of defeat. But when Cassius asks if this means that he is willing to be led in triumph as a captive, he replies "No! I can never submit to *that*." He has not thought of this possibility until Cassius suggests it, and then he admits that his philosophy is unequal to such a disgrace. He will kill himself rather than submit to it.

CASS.    For ever and for ever farewell, Brutus!
        If we do meet again, we'll smile indeed;      120
        If not, 'tis true this parting was well made.

BRU.    Why then, lead on. O that a man might know
        The end of this day's business ere it come!
        But it sufficeth that the day will end,
        And then the end is known. Come, ho! Away!    *Exeunt.* 125

### SCENE II. [*Near Philippi. The field of battle.*]†

*Alarum. Enter* Brutus *and* Messala.

BRU.    Ride, ride, Messala, ride, and give these bills
        Unto the legions on the other side.        *Loud alarum.*
        Let them set on at once; for I perceive
        But cold demeanour in Octavius' wing,
        And sudden push gives them the overthrow.      5
        Ride, ride, Messala! Let them all come down.    *Exeunt.*

### SCENE III. [*Another part of the field.*]

*Alarums. Enter* Cassius *and* Titinius.

CASS.    O, look, Titinius, look! The villains fly!
        Myself have to mine own turn'd enemy.
        This ensign here of mine was turning back;
        I slew the coward and did take it from him.

TIT.    O Cassius, Brutus gave the word too early,      5
        Who, having some advantage on Octavius,

---

123. **ere:** before. [S.H.]

**SCENE II.**

1. **bills:** papers, dispatches, written instructions. 2. **the other side:** the other wing of the army.—**alarum:** a trumpet sound calling to arms. 3. **set on:** attack. [S.H.] 4. **cold demeanor:** weak fighting spirit. [S.H.]

**SCENE III.**

1. **The villains:** here, his own troops. [S.H.] 2. **mine own:** my own men. 3-4. **ensign:** standard-bearer.— **it:** the ensign which he carried.

---

†     Some film versions take the opportunity to present spectacular fighting. This is notably the case of Burge's film in which numerous extras on foot or on horses fight in impressive *mêlée*s. In Bradley's film, the limited budget was compensated through the quick editing of brief shots showing shields against shields, swords against shields, close-ups of soldiers throwing spears, fighting, dying, cutting throats or falling. The end of the battle is a montage of dead soldiers trodden upon or agonizing in the sand. The shots put the stress on the human waste brought by the civil war. [S.H.]

Took it too eagerly. His soldiers fell to spoil,
Whilst we by Antony are all enclos'd.

*Enter* Pindarus.

PIN. Fly further off, my lord! fly further off!
Mark Antony is in your tents, my lord. 10
Fly, therefore, noble Cassius, fly far off!

CASS. This hill is far enough. Look, look, Titinius!
Are those my tents where I perceive the fire?

TIT. They are, my lord.

CASS.               Titinius, if thou lovest me,
Mount thou my horse and hide thy spurs in him 15
Till he have brought thee up to yonder troops
And here again, that I may rest assur'd
Whether yond troops are friend or enemy.

TIT. I will be here again even with a thought.    *Exit.*

CASS. Go, Pindarus, get higher on that hill. 20
My sight was ever thick. Regard Titinius,
And tell me what thou not'st about the field.   [Pindarus *goes up.*]
This day I breathed first.† Time is come round,
And where I did begin, there shall I end.
My life is run his compass. Sirrah, what news? 25

PIN. [*above*] O my lord!

CASS. What news?

PIN. [*above*] Titinius is enclosed round about
With horsemen that make to him on the spur.‡
Yet he spurs on. Now they are almost on him. 30

---

7. **fell to spoil:** started to loot. [S.H.] 11. **far:** probably "farther." [S.H.] 21. **thick:** indistinct, dim. This detail is from North's Plutarch: "His sight was very bad."—**Regard:** observe. 22. **not'st:** see, notice. [S.H.] 25. **his compass:** its circuit.—**Sirrah:** often used in familiar address, as to a servant or attendant. See note on 3.1.10. 26. **above:** on the upper stage. 29. **make to him on the spur:** approach him at full speed. [S.H.]

---

†   Cassius refers to his birthday. He notes that he was born (and had breathéd first) on this very day (years ago). [S.H.]

‡   In Bradley's boldest interpretation, the slave, Pindarus, makes a false report to Cassius. He watches Titinius (replaced by Decius in this version) being greeted by friends and not by enemies, but decides to lie to Cassius. After stabbing Cassius, Pindarus explodes with joy and runs away, having obtained his freedom. Burge's film gives a more classic interpretation. Though we do see Titinius riding toward the camp and being encircled by screaming horsemen, the images remain very ambiguous about the nature of those horsemen and do not give anything away. Pindarus is easily mistaken by what he witnesses. Mankiewicz's version retains the full ambiguity of the report as the sequence does not include any image of Titinius approaching the camp. [S.H.]

Now, Titinius!
Now some light. O, he lights too! He's ta'en. [*Shout.*] And hark!
They shout for joy.

CASS.                    Come down; behold no more.
O coward that I am to live so long
To see my best friend ta'en before my face!                                    35

*Enter* Pindarus [*from above*].

Come hither, sirrah.
In Parthia did I take thee prisoner;
And then I swore thee, saving of thy life,
That whatsoever I did bid thee do,
Thou shouldst attempt it. Come now, keep thine oath.             40
Now be a freeman, and with this good sword,
That ran through Caesar's bowels, search this bosom.
Stand not to answer. Here, take thou the hilts;
And when my face is cover'd, as 'tis now,
Guide thou the sword. [Pindarus *stabs him.*] —Caesar, thou art
    reveng'd                                                                          45
Even with the sword that kill'd thee.                              [*Dies.*]

PIN.    So, I am free; yet would not so have been,
Durst I have done my will. O Cassius!
Far from this country Pindarus shall run,
Where never Roman shall take note of him.                  [*Exit.*]  50

*Enter* Titinius *and* Messala.

MES.    It is but change, Titinius; for Octavius
Is overthrown by noble Brutus' power,
As Cassius' legions are by Antony.

TIT.    These tidings will well comfort Cassius.

MES.    Where did you leave him?

TIT.                         All disconsolate,                              55
With Pindarus his bondman, on this hill.

MES.    Is not that he that lies upon the ground?

TIT.    He lies not like the living. O my heart!

MES.    Is not that he?

---

31. **light:** alight, dismount. [S.H.] 35. **To see:** as to see. 38. **I swore thee:** I made you swear. [S.H.]—
**saving of thy life:** when I spared thy life. 42. **search:** probe. [S.H.] 43. **stand not to answer:** answer
rapidly. [S.H.] —**the hilts:** common in the plural, since the hilt of a sword consists of various parts. 47.
**would not so have been:** should not have chosen freedom on such conditions. 48. **Durst I:** if I dared.
[S.H.] 51. **change:** exchange. 52. **power:** army, troop. 54. **comfort:** hearten, encourage.

| | |
|---|---|
| Tit. | No, this was he, Messala, |
| | But Cassius is no more. O setting sun,      60 |
| | As in thy red rays thou dost sink to night, |
| | So in his red blood Cassius' day is set! |
| | The sun of Rome is set. Our day is gone; |
| | Clouds, dews, and dangers come; our deeds are done! |
| | Mistrust of my success hath done this deed.      65 |
| Mes. | Mistrust of good success hath done this deed. |
| | O hateful Error, Melancholy's child, |
| | Why dost thou show to the apt thoughts of men |
| | The things that are not? O Error, soon conceiv'd, |
| | Thou never com'st unto a happy birth,      70 |
| | But kill'st the mother that engend'red thee! |
| Tit. | What, Pindarus! Where art thou, Pindarus? |
| Mes. | Seek him, Titinius, whilst I go to meet |
| | The noble Brutus, thrusting this report |
| | Into his ears. I may say 'thrusting' it;      75 |
| | For piercing steel and darts envenomed |
| | Shall be as welcome to the ears of Brutus |
| | As tidings of this sight. |
| Tit. | Hie you, Messala, |
| | And I will seek for Pindarus the while.    [*Exit* Messala.] |
| | Why didst thou send me forth, brave Cassius?      80 |
| | Did I not meet thy friends, and did not they |
| | Put on my brows this wreath of victory |
| | And bid me give it thee? Didst thou not hear their shouts? |
| | Alas, thou hast misconstrued everything! |
| | But hold thee, take this garland on thy brow.      85 |
| | Thy Brutus bid me give it thee, and I |
| | Will do his bidding. Brutus, come apace |
| | And see how I regarded Caius Cassius. |
| | By your leave, gods. This is a Roman's part. |
| | Come, Cassius' sword, and find Titinius' heart.    *Dies.*  90 |

*Alarum. Enter* Brutus, Messala, Young Cato, Strato, Volumnius, *and* Lucilius.

---

65. **Mistrust of my success:** fear as to how I should succeed. *Succeed* and *success* are often used in a neutral sense. Cf. 2.2.6. *Good success* in the next line refers to the general outcome of the battle. 68. **apt:** ready (in this case, ready to entertain error). 71. **kill'st the mother:** as vipers were supposed to do. The mother of *Error* is *Melancholy,* and the error destroys the mind that conceives it; for it leads to the death or downfall of the person in question. Not a general truth, but general enough for Messala's mood of despair. 78. **Hie you:** Be quick. [S.H.] 85. **hold thee:** merely an interjection, like "hold" or "here." 89. **By your leave:** Titinius asks the permission of the gods to kill himself before the time which they have appointed.

| | | |
|---|---|---|
| BRU. | Where, where, Messala, doth his body lie? | |
| MES. | Lo, yonder, and Titinius mourning it. | |
| BRU. | Titinius' face is upward. | |
| CATO. | He is slain. | |
| BRU. | O Julius Caesar, thou art mighty yet! | |

BRU.      O Julius Caesar, thou art mighty yet!
          Thy spirit walks abroad and turns our swords                    95
          In our own proper entrails.                          *Low alarums.*

CATO.                              Brave Titinius!
          Look whe'r he have not crown'd dead Cassius.

BRU.      Are yet two Romans living such as these?
          The last of all the Romans, fare thee well!
          It is impossible that ever Rome                                 100
          Should breed thy fellow. Friends, I owe moe tears
          To this dead man than you shall see me pay.
          I shall find time, Cassius; I shall find time.
          Come therefore, and to Thasos send his body.
          His funerals shall not be in our camp,                          105
          Lest it discomfort us. Lucilius, come;
          And come, young Cato. Let us to the field.
          Labeo and Flavius set our battles on.
          'Tis three o'clock; and, Romans, yet ere night
          We shall try fortune in a second fight.              *Exeunt.* 110

SCENE IV. [*Another part of the field.*]†

*Alarum. Enter* Brutus, Messala, [Young] Cato, Lucilius, *and* Flavius.

BRU.      Yet, countrymen, O, yet hold up your heads!

CATO.     What bastard doth not? Who will go with me?
          I will proclaim my name about the field.

---

96. **In:** into.—**our own proper entrails:** *proper* simply emphasizes *own.* The Elizabethans could say *our own, our proper,* or *our own proper,* without real difference of meaning.—**Brave Titinius:** not "courageous," but "noble." 97. **whe'r:** whether. [S.H.] 101. **moe:** cf. 2.1.72. 104–106. **Thasos:** an island off the coast of Thrace, not far from Philippi. North's Plutarch records that Brutus sent the body of Cassius there "fearing least his funerals within the campe should cause great disorder."—**discomfort us:** dishearten our troops. 110. **a second fight:** The "second fight" at Philippi really took place twenty days after the first; but Shakespeare, as usual, has condensed the time for dramatic effect.

---

†    Under Burge's direction, the second part of the battle is marked by Caesar's revenge. As Brutus makes a final assault, images of Caesar's face delivering "Et tu, Brute?" are superimposed upon the battlefield, as if Brutus was, now more than ever, haunted by his past betrayal. [S.H.]

I am the son of Marcus Cato, ho!
A foe to tyrants, and my country's friend.                                5
I am the son of Marcus Cato, ho!

*Enter* Soldiers *and fight.*

LUCIL.    And I am Brutus, Marcus Brutus I!
Brutus, my country's friend! Know me for Brutus!        [*Exit.*]

[*Young* Cato *falls.*]

LUCIL.    O young and noble Cato, art thou down?
Why, now thou diest as bravely as Titinius,                      10
And mayst be honor'd, being Cato's son.

1. SOLD.    Yield, or thou diest.

LUCIL.                    Only I yield to die.
[*Offers money.*] There is so much that thou wilt kill me straight.
Kill Brutus, and be honor'd in his death.

1. SOLD.    We must not. A noble prisoner!                         15

*Enter* Antony.

2. SOLD.    Room ho! Tell Antony Brutus is ta'en.

1. SOLD.    I'll tell the news. Here comes the general.
Brutus is ta'en! Brutus is ta'en, my lord!

ANT.    Where is he?

LUCIL.    Safe, Antony; Brutus is safe enough.                     20
I dare assure thee that no enemy
Shall ever take alive the noble Brutus.
The gods defend him from so great a shame!
When you do find him, or alive or dead,
He will be found like Brutus, like himself.                        25

ANT.    This is not Brutus, friend; but, I assure you,
A prize no less in worth. Keep this man safe;
Give him all kindness. I had rather have
Such men my friends than enemies. Go on,
And see whe'r Brutus be alive or dead;                             30
And bring us word unto Octavius' tent
How every thing is chanc'd.                    *Exeunt.*

---

**SCENE IV.**

4. **Marcus Cato:** Cato of Utica. See note on 5.1.101. 10-11. **bravely:** nobly.—**mayst...son:** mayst receive
the honor which Cato's son should deserve and of which thou hast proved thyself worthy. 25. **like himself:**
true to himself. [S.H.] 30. **whe'r:** whether. [S.H.] 32. **is chanc'd:** has finally turned out. [S.H.]

SCENE V. [*Another part of the field.*]

*Enter* Brutus, Dardanius, Clitus, Strato, *and* Volumnius.

BRU.    Come, poor remains of friends, rest on this rock.

CLI.    Statilius show'd the torchlight; but, my lord,
        He came not back. He is or ta'en or slain.

BRU.    Sit thee down, Clitus. Slaying is the word.
        It is a deed in fashion. Hark thee, Clitus.          [*Whispers.*]    5

CLI.    What, I, my lord? No, not for all the world!

BRU.    Peace then. No words.

CLI.                            I'll rather kill myself.

BRU.    Hark thee, Dardanius.                                [*Whispers.*]

DAR.                            Shall I do such a deed?

CLI.    O Dardanius!

DAR.    O Clitus!                                                            10

CLI.    What ill request did Brutus make to thee?

DAR.    To kill him, Clitus. Look, he meditates.

CLI.    Now is that noble vessel full of grief,
        That it runs over even at his eyes.

BRU.    Come hither, good Volumnius. List a word.                           15

VOL.    What says my lord?

BRU.                            Why this, Volumnius.
        The ghost of Caesar hath appear'd to me
        Two several times by night—at Sardis once,
        And this last night here in Philippi fields.
        I know my hour is come.

VOL.                            Not so, my lord.                            20

BRU.    Nay, I am sure it is, Volumnius.
        Thou seest the world, Volumnius, how it goes.
        Our enemies have beat us to the pit.            *Low alarums.*

---

SCENE V.

13. **noble vessel**: the figure is Biblical. Cf. Romans, ix, 22: "What if God, willing to shew his wrath, and to make his power known, endured with much long-suffering the vessels of wrath fitted to destruction?"
15. **List a word:** listen to. [S.H.] 17. **The ghost of Caesar:** this settles the identity of the apparition in 4.3.
18. **several:** separate. [S.H.] 23. **the pit:** either "the abyss of destruction" or "the grave."

It is more worthy to leap in ourselves
Than tarry till they push us. Good Volumnius,       25
Thou know'st that we two went to school together.
Even for that our love of old, I prithee
Hold thou my sword-hilts whilst I run on it.

VOL.   That's not an office for a friend, my lord.        *Alarum still.*

CLI.   Fly, fly, my lord! There is no tarrying here.       30

BRU.   Farewell to you; and you; and you, Volumnius.
Strato, thou hast been all this while asleep.
Farewell to thee too, Strato. Countrymen,
My heart doth joy that yet in all my life
I found no man but he was true to me.        35
I shall have glory by this losing day
More than Octavius and Mark Antony
By this vile conquest shall attain unto.
So fare you well at once; for Brutus' tongue
Hath almost ended his live's history.        40
Night hangs upon mine eyes; my bones would rest,
That have but labor'd to attain this hour.
                            *Alarum. Cry within*: Fly, fly, fly!

CLI.   Fly, my lord, fly!

BRU.              Hence! I will follow.

       [*Exeunt* Clitus, Dardanius, *and* Volumnius.]
I prithee, Strato, stay thou by thy lord.
Thou art a fellow of a good respect;        45
Thy life hath had some smatch of honor in it.
Hold then my sword, and turn away thy face
While I do run upon it. Wilt thou, Strato?

STRA.  Give me your hand first. Fare you well, my lord.

---

26. **school:** This pathetic touch is from Plutarch. But Shakespeare himself often brings in allusions to the memories of schooldays. One notable instance occurs in 1.2.300. 28. **sword-hilts:** cf. 5.3.43. 34. **joy:** rejoice. [S.H.] 38. **vile:** in the eyes of Brutus, the victory of Octavius and Antony is the final downfall of Roman freedom. Not for a moment does he doubt the justice of his own cause or the nobility of his action in killing Caesar. 40. **live's:** a common form for the genitive of *life.* 42. **this hour:** the hour of rest and death. Death is no calamity according to the Stoic belief of Brutus, but, if nobly attained, a rest from the evils of life. 45. **respect:** reputation. 46. **some smatch:** some relish or taste. A by-form of *smack*—not a vulgarism in Shakespeare's time.

BRU.            Farewell, good Strato. Caesar, now be still.                    50
                I kill'd not thee with half so good a will.
                                [*He runs on his sword and dies.*]†

*Alarum. Retreat. Enter* Octavius, Antony, Messala, Lucilius, *and the* Army.

OCT.            What man is that?

MES.            My master's man. Strato, where is thy master?

STRA.           Free from the bondage you are in, Messala.
                The conquerors can but make a fire of him;            55
                For Brutus only overcame himself,
                And no man else hath honor by his death.

LUCIL.          So Brutus should be found. I thank thee, Brutus,
                That thou hast prov'd Lucilius' saying true.

OCT.            All that serv'd Brutus, I will entertain them.           60
                Fellow, wilt thou bestow thy time with me?

STRA.           Ay, if Messala will prefer me to you.

OCT.            Do so, good Messala.

MES.            How died my master, Strato?

STRA.           I held the sword, and he did run on it.                  65

MES.            Octavius, then take him to follow thee,
                That did the latest service to my master.

ANT.            This was the noblest Roman of them all.
                All the conspirators save only he
                Did that they did in envy of great Caesar;              70
                He, only in a general honest thought
                And common good to all, made one of them.
                His life was gentle, and the elements

---

50. **Caesar, now be still:** rest, perturbed spirit; for thou art avenged by this sacrifice which I make of myself. It was a common belief that the spirits of the dead were restless if unavenged. 56. **only:** alone. [S.H.] 59. **Lucilius' saying:** i.e., the prediction in 5.4.21-25. 60. **entertain them:** take them into my service. 61. **bestow:** employ. 62. **prefer:** recommend. 71-72. **in a general honest thought And common good to all:** with a universally honorable purpose (unmixed with selfish considerations), and for the sake of the good of all the Romans in common.

---

†    At this point, Bradley's film makes us share Brutus's subjective vision as he runs toward his sword. But we do not see the actual impaling because, at this very moment, the film cuts to the Ghost of Caesar's face, grinning slightly. This shot puts the stress on Caesar's revenge, as if it was Caesar himself who was holding the sword and was then satisfied with the killing. Mankiewicz's, Burge's and the BBC's versions have chosen to emphasize the homoerotic aspect of the suicide as Brutus agonizes in the arms of Strato. [S.H.]

So mix'd in him that Nature might stand up
And say to all the world, 'This was a man!'†                75

OCT.    According to his virtue let us use him,
With all respect and rites of burial.
Within my tent his bones tonight shall lie,
Most like a soldier, ordered honorably.
So call the field to rest, and let's away
To part the glories of this happy day.                *Exeunt omnes.*

---

79. **ordered honorably:** treated with all due honor. 81. **part:** divide, share out. [S.H.]

---

†    The versions made for the cinema all end with these words spoken by Antony, as they convey the greatest sense of closure. In Bradley's film, the camera tracks back to reveal Antony and Octavius standing on a hill on each side of Brutus's body. In a chiaroscuro lighting, the film ends with a romantic homage to a heroic Brutus. Mankiewicz preferred to end with an intimate rather than an epic shot: the camera tracks forward onto Brutus's face in profile, as he lies within his tent. [S.H.]

# How to Read
## *Julius Caesar* as Performance

"How many ages hence/ Shall this our lofty scene be acted over/ In states unborn and accents yet unknown!" (3.1). This is how Cassius reacts after having taken part in the murder of Caesar with all the other conspirators. The play makes here a direct reference to the theater, the medium for which it has been written. The characters in the play often reveal that they are actors playing parts. When Brutus advises his fellow conspirators, he urges them to conduct the affair as efficiently as actors would do: "Let not our looks put on our purposes,/ But bear it as our Roman actors do,/ With untir'd spirits and formal constancy" (2.1). When Cassius meditates on his relationship with Brutus, he shifts roles as if he were a director allowed to redistribute the parts in the play: "If I were Brutus now and he were Cassius,/ He should not humor me" (1.2). As you read the play, you will often be reminded by Shakespeare that what you are reading is a play-script meant to be performed.

Such a text that keeps reflecting on the medium of theater was, in fact, written for a very specific system of performance, one that regularly disclosed the illusion of acting. At the end of the sixteenth century and the start of the seventeenth, Elizabethan popular plays were performed on an open-air stage, during the day, in a circular or polygonal construction in which the spectators stood in the stalls or sat in the galleries. All parts were played exclusively by male actors who occupied a bare stage where space and time were suggested only in a verbal way. This absence of a realistic frame avoided the need of changing sets between scenes. In the case of *Julius Caesar*, it was, therefore, very easy to move from Brutus's house to the Capitol, from the Capitol to the Forum, and finally to the plains of Philippi where the battle takes place. Acting was continuous, and the scenes followed one after the other with fluid rapidity. Visual aids to imagination were minimal and inherent in the architecture of public theaters: a roof painted above the stage represented the sky and the divine; a trap door under the floor could evoke hell. No set designs were created to represent views of Rome or the landscapes at Philippi.

In Shakespeare's time, the presentation of the plays showed, therefore, a constant distancing between what is seen and what is said, as well as an absence of illusionist intention. The Elizabethan public theater, with its thrust stage, established a privileged relationship with the audience on three sides nearly encircling the action. Most spectators saw the play being performed in a setting composed of other spectators. The audience attended both the play and the stage activity surrounding and creating the play. The boundary was blurred between art and life, between the actor and the spectator: both were united in the same communion of entertainment and imagination. Elizabethan drama played with the spectators and their permanent awareness of theatrical illusion. The actors' soliloquies and asides, like Brutus's monologue when he ponders Caesar's murder in 2.1 or Antony's prophecy over Caesar's dead body in 3.1, were conventions that established intimacy with the public while signaling the devices of theater (as talking to oneself aloud is more a stage convention than a natural practice). The spectators intervened regularly during the performance, participating in the action with their own reactions. You can imagine easily how a play like *Julius Caesar* benefited from such an environment. During the Forum scene (3.2), spectators could add their own shouts to the Roman people's exclamations. They could support Brutus or Mark Antony with their booing or cheering. The audience at the Globe theater (for which Shakespeare's *Julius Caesar* was written in 1599) could become part of the Roman crowd, totally immersed in the dramatic events.

Shakespeare's playtexts regularly refer to the theater, but they do not include many stage directions. They differ greatly from plays written in the nineteenth and twentieth centuries by playwrights such as Henrik Ibsen, Arthur Miller or Eugene O'Neill. These plays usually include numerous stage directions that describe precisely the setting as well as the characters' behaviors and emotions. Such dramas are, in a way, accompanied by their own commentary guiding the forthcoming performances. They seem to carry within themselves the very setting in situation of their dialogues. By contrast, if one excludes the few stage directions generally indicating the characters' entrances and exits, Shakespeare's playtexts are mainly composed of dialogues and monologues (even though some Quarto versions are slightly more abundant in terms of stage directions).

When you read a play, you should, therefore, try and play with your imagination to give flesh to the text as if you were seeing everything happening before you. You can choose to read the text immediately or to look for some assistance before starting—you can either read a plot summary to help you grasp the story or see a film production of the play that will provide you with the subjective vision of a director.

Once you start reading, you will have to create an inner show for yourself as if you were a theater or film director. You can decide to view the show as if it was performed on a stage or as a piece of cinema. But in both cases, you will have to imagine the setting, what the actors look like, how they are dressed, how they move and how they speak. The way a line is pronounced can influence the meaning of the text. Let us take the example of a line Antony speaks during his Forum speech as he reveals Caesar's wounds and the holes made by the daggers in his toga: "This was the most unkindest cut of all" (3.2.174). If you imagine that Antony stresses the first word "This," then the line could draw attention to Antony showing a hole with a spectacular gesture, emphasizing the wounded body he displays in front of the crowd.

If the stress is on "unkindest," what will be highlighted is the conspirators' cruelty when they stabbed Caesar. If now the stress is on "cut," the violent act of stabbing itself is given more prominence. You, as a reader, must decide what word(s) you will pick to be the core(s) of each line in order to create your own personal intonation. As you read through the play, do not fear the lack of stage directions. On the contrary, consider it as a series of opportunities. For you can decide for yourself what kind of additional subtext you will weave around Shakespeare's dialogues and monologues. When you read a scene, imagine how it could be performed. Are the characters sincere or hypocritical when they speak their lines? Are they ironic? What is their status in society? Why are they speaking these lines? What are their hidden motives? What are they trying to obtain? What gestures or moves come with their speech?

If you choose to imagine the play as performed on stage, try and envisage how the audience might react at the hearing of certain scenes. Could they be afraid, amused or simply moved? In your own version of *Julius Caesar*, would they feel for Caesar's tragic fate, or identify with Brutus's upsetting dilemma?

If you decide to imagine the play as a piece of cinema, you have to place yourself behind the virtual eye of a film camera. In the cinema, as in the Elizabethan theaters, scenes move on with great rapidity and fluidity. Through editing, film, like a theater production in Shakespeare's time, can move quickly from the private discussion between Cassius and Brutus in a tent, to the battle scene in the plains of Philippi. However, cinema differs from Elizabethan public theaters because of the high level of realism it can reach (you can, therefore, start imagining magnificent exterior settings for Rome, Sardis and Philippi). Moreover, while the architecture of the Elizabethan theaters allowed the spectators to see the action from different angles, cinema offers a single frontal viewpoint, and through editing and camera moves, mandates how the action will be seen.

A movie is usually made in three stages. The first stage can be compared to theatrical organization and organizes what takes place in front of the camera (acting, *mise-en-scène*, setting). The second stage concerns the actual camerawork during the shooting—it is a framing process. Then, during the third stage, the filmed images are linked together—an assembling and editing process. By giving the film director the possibility of alternating points of view during the unfolding of events, editing manages the quantity of information given to the audience. Directors can concentrate the attention of spectators in turn on the various characters, on their perceptions and reactions. When you read each scene of the play, you can thus pick up the moments when you would allow the characters some close-ups that would reveal their reactions and emotions. Try and decide how you would film the quarrel opposing Brutus and Cassius in the fourth act. Would you show Cassius's outraged expression when Brutus utters his accusations? Or would you rather focus on Brutus's angry look? Would you film the two characters in one single shot or in separate shots linked with montage? Again, the possibilities for creating your own show are endless.

In 5.3, Cassius asks his slave Pindarus to go up a hill and report what he sees of Titinius's approach toward their military camp. Pindarus reports that Titinius is encircled and soon taken. Cassius is despairing and commits suicide, helped by Pindarus. Later, we learn that Titinius was surrounded by friends, not by enemies. Cassius has killed himself because of a tragic misunderstanding. When you read this episode, you can choose to visualize what Pindarus really sees. Is he making the mistake himself, truthfully thinking that Titinius has been captured by enemies? Or is he reporting ambiguous news on purpose, certain as he is that his master will kill himself and free him? This last interpretation was, for example, chosen by David Bradley in his 1950 film. When you read a speech that gives the report of an event (such as Casca's tale of Caesar's refusal of the coronet in 1.2, for example), ask yourself if the character might not offer a distorted vision of reality in order to serve his personal goals.

As you discover Shakespeare's *Julius Caesar,* you should see it as a real challenge for your abilities to interpret it and flesh it out. But whatever you decide, you should always bear in mind that Shakespeare does not make any clear choices but maintains ambiguity or ambivalence wherever possible. This is what makes his plays difficult but also rich, complex and rewarding once you know how to grasp the multiple meanings they can convey.

# TIMELINE

B.C. 753: Mythical founding of Rome by Romulus and Remus.

B.C. 509: Rome becomes a republic when Junius Brutus overthrows King Tarquin the Proud.

B.C. 264-146: Punic wars between Rome and Catharge.

B.C. 100-102: Gaius Julius Caesar born (by Caesarean section according to an unlikely legend) of Aurelia and Gaius Julius Caesar, a praetor.

B.C. 78: Caesar began a career as an orator/lawyer (throughout his life he was known as an eloquent speaker).

B.C. 73-71: Slave revolt led by gladiator Spartacus.

B.C. 68-67: Caesar obtained a seat in the Senate. He supported Gnaeus Pompey and helped him get an extraordinary generalship against the Mediterranean pirates.

B.C. 60: Caesar joins with Pompey and Crassus in a loose coalition called the First Triumvirate.

B.C. 59: Caesar elected consul. He marries Calphurnia, the daughter of a leading politician. His only daughter, Julia (born from a previous marriage), is married to Pompey to consolidate their alliance.

B.C. 58: Caesar leaves Rome for Gaul (current-day France) and starts the conquest of most of what is now central Europe, opening up these lands to Mediterranean civilization.

B.C. 54: Caesar leads a three-month expedition to Britain (this was the first Roman crossing of the English Channel), but did not establish a permanent base there. His coalition with Pompey is increasingly strained, especially after Julia dies in childbirth.

B.C. 53: Crassus receives command of the armies of the East but is defeated and killed by the Parthians.

B.C. 49: A civil war starts between Caesar and Pompey. Caesar crosses the Rubicon river (the border of his province) with his army. He quickly advances to Rome and has himself declared dictator. Throughout his campaign, Caesar practices with much publicity a policy of clemency (putting no one to death and confiscating no property).

B.C. 48:   Caesar beats Pompey in the plains of Pharsalus (Greece), though the toll is great on both sides; Caesar pardons all Roman citizens who are captured, including Brutus, but Pompey escapes and flees to Egypt.

B.C. 48, October: Caesar lands in Alexandria and is presented, to his professed horror, with the head of Pompey, who has been betrayed by the Egyptians. Caesar decides to support Cleopatra's right to the Egyptian throne against her brother Ptolemy. With 4,000 legionaries, he manages to hold the palace and the harbor against an army of 20,000 men. Unfortunately, during the fight, the great Library of Alexandria accidentally burns down.

B.C. 47, March: Thanks to military reinforcement, Caesar defeats the Egyptian army. He remains in Egypt until June, even cruising on the Nile with Cleopatra to the southern boundary of her kingdom.

B.C. 47, June: Caesar leaves Alexandria, having established Cleopatra as a ruler in alliance with Rome; he also leaves three legions under the command of Rufio, as legate. Either immediately before or soon after he leaves Egypt, Cleopatra gives birth to a son that she names Caesarion, claiming that he is Caesar's son.

B.C. 47:   Caesar sweeps through Asia Minor to settle the disturbances there. On August 1, he meets and immediately overcomes Pharnaces, a rebellious king; he will later publicize the rapidity of this victory with the slogan *veni, vidi, vici* ("I came, I saw, I overcame").

B.C. 46:   Back to Rome, Caesar sends for Cleopatra and Caesarion, and establishes them in a luxurious villa. Holding the position of dictator, Caesar governs autocratically—although he uses the political structure, he often simply announces his decisions to the Senate without debate or vote.

B.C. 45, April: The two sons of Pompey, Gnaeus and Sextus, lead a revolt in Spain. Caesar wins a decisive but difficult victory at Munda. Gnaeus Pompey is killed in the battle, but Sextus escapes to become, later, the leader of the Mediterranean pirates.

B.C. 45, October: Caesar, back in Rome, celebrates a triumph over Gnaeus Pompey, arousing discontent because triumphs were reserved for victories against foreign enemies. By this time, Caesar virtually appoints all major magistrates, issues coins with his likeness and allows his statues to be adorned like the statues of the gods. The Senate also constantly votes him new honors—the right to wear the laurel wreath and purple and gold toga and sit in a gilded chair at all public functions, etc. When two tribunes, Gaius Marullus and Lucius Flavius, oppose these measures, Caesar has them removed from office and from the Senate.

B.C. 44, February: Caesar is named *dictator perpetuus* (dictator for life). On February 15, at the feast of Lupercalia, Caesar wears his purple garb for the first time in public. At the public festival, Antony offers him a diadem but Caesar refuses it, saying that Jupiter alone is king of the Romans (possibly because he understands that the people do not want him to accept the diadem, or possibly because he wants to end once and for all the speculation that he is trying to become a king).

B.C. 44, March 15th: Caesar attends a meeting of the Senate held at its temporary quarters in the portico of the theater built by Pompey (the regular meeting house of the Senate had been badly burned and was being rebuilt). The conspirators, led by Marcus Junius Brutus, Gaius Cassius Longinus, Decimus Brutus Albinus, and Gaius Trebonius, come to the meeting with daggers concealed in their togas and strike Caesar at least 23 times as he stand at the base of Pompey's statue. Legend has it that Caesar said in Greek to Brutus, "You, too, my child?" After Caesar's assassination, Mark Antony allies with Octavius and Lepidus to form the Second Triumvirate.

B.C. 42: Octavius and Antony march their army toward Brutus and Cassius. After two engagements at the battle of Philippi, during the first of which Cassius commits suicide (October 3rd), Brutus flees with his remaining forces. Seeing that defeat and capture is imminent, he commits suicide by falling on his sword (October 23rd).

B.C. 33: The Second Triumvirate breaks up.

B.C. 31: In the ensuing civil war Antony is defeated by Octavius at the battle of Actium (Greece) and then at Alexandria. He commits suicide along with his lover, Queen Cleopatra. Octavius thus becomes the sole ruler of Rome and accepts the surname Augustus.

46: Plutarch born in the Greek region of Boeotia. He will become an influential Greek philosopher and author, well known for his biographies and his moral treatises. His best-known work is the *Parallel Lives*, a series of biographies of famous Greeks and Romans (including Cicero, Crassus, Pompey, Julius Caesar, Mark Antony and Brutus), which attempt to illuminate their common moral virtues or failings.

1564: William Shakespeare born in Stratford-upon-Avon to John and Mary Shakespeare

1567: The opening of the Red Lion Playhouse, the first public playhouse in England.

1576: James Burbage and his family build The Theater, long thought to be the first public playhouse.

1579: The first edition of Sir Thomas North's translation of Plutarch's *Lives*, from the French of Jacques Amyot, is released. This first edition is dedicated to Queen Elizabeth.

1582: William Shakespeare marries Anne Hatthaway.

1583:   Birth of Shakespeare's daughter, Susanna.

1585:   Birth of Shakespeare's son, Hamnet, and daughter, Judith.

1592-94: Plague years. Theaters closed. Shakespeare wrote his poems and many of his sonnets during this period.

1594:   William Shakespeare and Richard Burbage become sharers in the Lord Chamberlain's Men, a company of actors, reorganized when the theatres reopen after the Plague. Shakespeare would later become a major shareholder in the theater and this, rather than publication of his plays, is how he made his money.

1596:   Burial of Hamnet Shakespeare, August 11th, in Stratford.

1599-1601: *Julius Caesar* has been thought to be the first play staged at the newly erected Globe Theater. Shakespeare also writes *Henry V* and *Hamlet* (a play which includes references to *Julius Caesar*).

1603:   Death of Elizabeth. James VI of Scotland (b. 1566) crowned King James I of England. The Lord Chamberlain's Men, recognized as the premier acting troupe in England, become the King's Men.

c.1611:  Shakespeare retires to Stratford.

1616, April 23rd: Death of William Shakespeare.

1623:   Publication of the *First Folio* containing most of Shakespeare's plays.

# Topics for Discussion and Further Study

## Critical Issues

1. Why do you think Shakespeare set Caesar's triumph at the same time as the Lupercal ceremonies? Look for information on this specific feast and ask yourself how it relates to the play's structure and themes.
2. Look for the numerous signs and prophecies that anticipate tragic events. What is considered as a sign in the play? How are the signs read? Are they wrongly or rightly interpreted? Will the events prove them right or wrong? Look for information on Elizabethan beliefs on prophecies and the supernatural.
3. Study the various scenes in which characters try to convince others and analyse the different strategies of persuasion. Which are effective and why?
4. Do you think that the murder of Caesar is justified? What elements in the play could appear against or in favor of Caesar's assassination? Is Caesar presented as a tyrant?
5. Look for the various occurrences of the words "blood" and "bloody" and examine how their meanings can evolve from scene to scene. What does that tell you about the status of words in the play?
6. Compare Brutus's and Antony's Forum speeches. What kind of rhetoric do they use? Which is the most efficient and why? Explore specifically the imagery and metaphors present in Antony's speech. What kind of Caesar is constructed in Brutus's speech and in Antony's speech? What does this tell you about Shakespeare's ambivalent drama?
7. Examine carefully the scenes featuring Calphurnia and Portia. How are women represented in the play? What are their roles? What are they trying to do? Are they presented in the same way?
8. What is, in your opinion, the function of the "Cinna the Poet" scene? Why did Shakespeare choose to include such a scene? What does it tell the audience about Caesar? About the conspirators? Why do you think it has often been cut in performance?

9. Explore the process of decision-making in the play. Who, between Cassius and Brutus, makes the decisions? Why? To what effect? What does it tell us about each character, their motives and their fate?

10. Notice how many events are told rather than shown. How is the Battle of Philippi represented, for example? And Caesar's refusal of the coronet? Why do you think Shakespeare chose to have some events reported rather than staged in front of the audience?

## Performance Issues

1. Imagine that you are directing *Julius Caesar* for the screen. You can pick among any actors you know to play the different parts. Who would you cast as Caesar, Brutus, Antony, Cassius, Portia and Calphurnia? Justify your choice by explaining your vision of each role.

2. This time, imagine that you are directing the play for the stage. How will you represent the Roman people at the Forum scene? Will you choose to have recorded voices coming from microphones? Will you hire many extras? Will you place some actors inside the theater audience? Justify your choice and explain what kind of effect you would like to achieve.

3. Find a scene that has been left out of one of the screen adaptations. Why do you think the director chose to cut it? For what consequence on the play's meaning? If the scene is included in another screen version, discuss the differences that result.

4. Choose a scene that appears in at least two different screen versions. Compare the sequences in terms of *mise-en-scène* (set design, actors' gestures and moves, vocal intonations), camera and sound work, editing, music, etc. What are, in each case, the consequences of all those decisions? What kind of emotions do the scenes try to convey? What is your favorite treatment of the sequence? Why?

5. Is there a film version that encourages you to feel more sympathy toward Antony? Toward Brutus? Toward Caesar? Try and discover what specific choices (in terms of film aesthetics or textual decisions) influence your sympathies.

6. In which specific film genre does Joseph Mankiewicz locate his *Julius Caesar* (1953)? Do you think placing a film into a certain genre is important? Why? Study the casting in the Mankiewicz version and in the Stuart Burge version (1970). What can you say about each casting? What is the effect on the audience's expectations?

7. If possible, watch the first part of *Cleopatra* (1963). How does director Joseph Mankiewicz present the conspiracy against Caesar and the murder scene? What does he show and what does he leave out? To what effect? Why do you think the director decided not to use Shakespeare's text for this adaptation, contrary to his version of *Julius Caesar* in 1953? What are the consequences of the two textual strategies?

8. Try and find some information on the context in which the screen versions were made (historical and political situation, economic constraints, etc.). How has the context influenced each film's vision of the play?

# BIBLIOGRAPHY

**Editor's note:** This bibliography includes both classic and recent works of scholarship that are easily accessible to advanced high school and college students. The bibliography offers diverse theoretical approaches and methodologies. In all cases, I have attempted to list some of the richest and most influential books and articles that will help students enrich their knowledge and vision of *Julius Caesar*. [S.H.]

Charney, Maurice. *Shakespeare's Roman Plays. The Function of Imagery in Drama.* Cambridge: Harvard University Press, 1961.

Charney notably studies the verbal imagery in Julius Caesar, such as the frequent talk of blood, but also the nonverbal dramatic effects which are not found in the poetic lines themselves, i.e. the theatrical expression or interpretation of the lines.

Crowl, Samuel. "A World Elsewhere: The Roman Plays on Film and Television" in *Shakespeare and the Moving Image, the plays on film and television.* Anthony Davies and Stanley Wells, eds. Cambridge: Cambridge University Press, 1994, 146-161.

One of the rare studies focusing on the screen adaptations of the Roman plays.

Foakes, R.A. "An Approach to Julius Caesar." *Shakespeare Quarterly* 5:3 (1954): 259-270.

A seminal article that studies the play's unity in its dramatic imagery, circular structure and pervading themes (blood and fire).

Khan, Coppélia. *Roman Shakespeare: Warriors, Wounds, and Women.* London and New York: Routledge, 1997.

Khan analyses how Shakespeare represents gender in the Roman plays. She explores "masculinity" as a specifically Roman cultural construction through the notion of virtus (that she links to heroism and emulation). "Feminity" is associated with chastity, a virtue that made women valuable in the social system of Rome. Kahn carefully shows how the character of Portia is constructed as a being combining the best qualities of both genders.

Knight, G. Wilson. *The Imperial Theme: Further Interpretations of Shakespeare's Tragedies including the Roman Plays*. London: Methuen & Co, 1951.

Knight studies the metaphors and symbols in the plays. He notably focuses on the themes of love and friendship in *Julius Caesar*.

Leggatt, Alexander. *Shakespeare's Political Drama: The History Plays and the Roman Plays*. London and New York: Routledge, 1988.

Leggatt discusses how the gaining (or losing) of public power is linked with play-acting. The volume includes a whole chapter devoted to *Julius Caesar*.

Liebler, Naomi Conn. "Thou bleeding Piece of Earth. The Ritual Ground of Julius Caesar." *Shakespeare Studies* 14 (1981): 175-96.

This article deals with the significance of the Lupercale as a fertility rite. In the play, Caesar appears to be afraid of sterility (i.e., sterile women such as Calphurnia, but also wastelands).

Miles, Geoffrey. *Shakespeare and the Constant Romans*. New York: Oxford University Press, 1996.

Miles offers an excellent study of the Stoic philosophy at work, notably in *Julius Caesar*. He explores the constant Brutus and the inconstant Antony in the play.

Miola, Robert S. "*Julius Caesar* and the Tyrannicide Debate." *Renaissance Quarterly* 38:2 (1985): 271-289.

Miola revisits the play in the light of the Reformation context. At various times, Protestants and Catholics challenged the authority of the crown and claimed the right of deposition and tyrannicide. Miola examines the meaning of the word "tyrant" in the play and examines the question of the assassination of the despotic ruler. This issue greatly preoccupied the England of Shakespeare's time in a political and religious context that attempted to encourage passive obedience and condemned civil strife.

Nettles, John. "Brutus in *Julius Caesar*." In *Players of Shakespeare 4*, ed. Robert Smallwood, 177-92. Cambridge: Cambridge University Press, 1998.

Nettles, who played Brutus for the Royal Shakespeare Company, sees this character as exhibiting two personae – public and private, the private being more honest and thus more sympathetic than the public.

Parker, Barbara L. "The Whore of Babylon and Shakespeare's *Julius Caesar*." *Studies in English Literature* 35:2 (1995): 251-269.

> Parker examines the numerous sexual metaphors in the play, arguing that Rome embodies whorish and unnatural love.

Paster, Gail Kern. "'In the Spirit of Men there is no Blood': Blood as Trope of Gender in *Julius Caesar*." *Shakespeare Quarterly* 40:3 (1989): 284-298.

> Paster explores the gender-specific meanings of blood and bleeding in the play by taking into account Renaissance anatomy and physiology. The assassination discloses the shameful secret of Caesar's bodiliness: a womanly inability to stop involuntary bleeding. On the contrary, Portia proves herself manly as she shows Brutus she can bear a voluntary wound in her thigh.

Rabkin, Norman. *Shakespeare and the Common Understanding*. New York: The Free Press, 1967.

> In the third chapter of this book, Rabkin studies the contradiction in the structure of the plays of *Coriolanus*, *Julius Caesar* and *Richard II*. He shows how Shakespeare dramatizes opposite views in the theories of kingship (which preceded the Puritan revolution) to show the complimentary validity of both.

Ripley, John. *"Julius Caesar" on stage in England & America, 1599-1973*. Cambridge: Cambridge University Press, 1980.

> Ripley has consulted many sources such as theater reviews and prompt-books to provide an extremely detailed account of the play in performance during four centuries.

Spencer, T.J.B. "Shakespeare and the Elizabethan Romans." *Shakespeare Survey* 10 (1957): 27-38.

> Spencer traces to what extent Shakespeare was in step with ideas about ancient Rome among his contemporaries and to what extent (and why) he diverged from them. After surveying the Elizabethan writing about Rome, Spencer concludes that, in Shakespeare's three principal Roman plays, we witness a steadily advancing independence of thought in the reconsideration of the Roman world.

Thomas, Vivian. *Julius Caesar. Harvester New Critical Introduction to Shakespeare*. New York: Twayne Publishers, 1992.

> This book examines the political, historical and tragic dimensions of the play. It focuses on the creation of a distinctively Roman world by Shakespeare, before assessing the different generic perceptions of the play. Particular attention is given to Shakespeare's sources.

Traversi, Derek. *Shakespeare: The Roman Plays*. Stanford, California: Stanford University Press, 1963.

> This volume includes a whole chapter on *Julius Caesar*, which offers a very detailed examination of the main characters' mixed motives.

Vawter, Marvin L. "'Division 'tween Our Souls': Shakespeare's Stoic Brutus." *Shakespeare Studies* 7 (1974): 173-195.

> A study of Brutus's Stoic philosophy. Vawter points out that, in Shakespeare's time, one of the sources of knowledge about Stoicism was *De Finibus,* in which Cicero, addressing Brutus, attacks this philosophy. Cicero's main point is that the Stoics were simply wrong about human nature: stoicism would be dangerous, as those who practice it become coldly inhumane.

Zander, Horst. *Julius Caesar: New Critical Essays*. New York: Routledge, 2005.

> This very complete collection of essays first surveys traditional approaches to the play (in the context of Renaissance England, in relation to Shakespeare's other Roman plays and in terms of structure, language, character, and source material). It then examines more recent debates concerning the play in Marxist, psychoanalytic, deconstructive, and gender contexts before exploring the play on stage.

# FILMOGRAPHY

*Julius Caesar* (1950). Dir. David Bradley. With David Bradley, Charlton Heston, Harold Tasker. 106 minutes. B & W. DVD release: July 2006. DVD Extras: Photo gallery, Trailer, "Beware the Ides of March": an analysis of Marc Anthony's Funeral Speech.

In this independent, low-budget production, Bradley proved very creative, using Expressionist cinematic techniques with chiaroscuro effects, extreme close-ups and imaginative editing. In his first professional role in the cinema, Charlton Heston plays a youthful and commanding Antony.

*Julius Caesar* (1953). Dir. Joseph L. Mankiewicz. With Marlon Brando, James Mason, John Gielgud, Louis Calhern, Greer Garson, Deborah Kerr. 120 minutes. B & W. DVD release: November 2006.

Mankiewicz shot this *Caesar* in typical Hollywood epic style, with numerous extras and spectacular scenes (especially the Forum sequence). This film is famous for blending the English and American styles of acting. Marlon Brando gives a memorable performance as Antony.

*Julius Caesar* (1970). Dir. Stuart Burge. With Charlton Heston, Jason Robards, John Gielgud, Robert Vaughn, Richard Chamberlain, Diana Rigg, Jill Bennet, Christopher Lee. 117 minutes. Color. DVD release: for the Pan & Scan version, May 2004; for the widescreen version: to be announced soon.

Burge gathered an impressive cast for the first color treatment of the play in the cinema. Though shot in the epic style, the film sometimes lacks some cinematic creativity and buoyancy.

*Julius Caesar* (1979). Dir. Herbert Wise. With Richard Pasco, Charles Gray, Keith Michell, David Collings, Virginia McKenna, Elizabeth Spriggs. 161 minutes. Color. The DVD can be bought separately, as part of the BBC Shakespeare Tragedies DVD Giftbox (released in 2002) or as part of the BBC TV Shakespeare Complete Collection (released in 2005).

This production was shot for television with a theater-related, non-realistic set. It is much more complete and faithful to the text than the previous screen version, and offers some very subtle acting and powerful moments.

*Julius Caesar* (2003). Dir. Uli Edel. With Jeremy Sisto, Richard Harris, Christopher Walken, Valeria Golino, Chris Noth. 270 minutes. Color. DVD release: October 2004.

In this TV film, Shakespeare's text is not used, but this is a useful production to revise Caesar's personal, military and political life in an entertaining way.

*Cleopatra* (1963). Dir. Joseph L. Mankiewicz. With Elizabeth Taylor, Richard Burton, Rex Harrison. 246 minutes. Color. DVD release: April 2001.

In this huge, long and famously expensive epic movie, Mankiewicz rewrites Shakespeare and, in the first part of the film, provides the viewers with Caesar's story, from his affair with Cleopatra to his death in the Capitol.